the 1984 Scout

Edited by Ron Jeffries

Contents

Our front cover shows Gary Howard winning a friendly race at Gilwell Park, the Scouts' National Camp Site on the edge of London's Epping Forest. Close behind are Karl Davis and Jeremy Squibb – and all three are Members of the 3rd Enfield Air Scout Troop. (Photograph by Julian Simmonds.) **The inset photograph shows John Craven, of BBC TV's *Newsround* fame, with Ali Catterall and Paul Rymer of the 15th Chelsea Scout Troop** (and you can read more about them on page 38). (Photograph by Ted Gatt.) **The main illustration on the back cover is detail from 'Kielder – The Place' which appears on pages 32 and 33.** (Illustration by Bill Bruce.) **The inset photographs show Paul McGarry and David Pickworth – both of the Merlin Patrol, 28th Leicester** (Wigston) **Tythorn Scout Troop – setting out on the hike that features on page 54 onwards** (photograph by Dave Siddons); **the second photograph has Paul Payne, Mark Hughes and Mark Roberts of the 1st Bishops Cleeve – who helped with 'Camp Food – Glorious Food!' on page 12** (photograph by John Elliott).

World
Published in Great Britain by World International Publishing Limited.
A Pentos Company.
P. O. Box 111, Great Ducie Street, Manchester M60 3BL.
Printed in Belgium.
SBN 7235 6678 X

EMERGENCY!

David Saint
Illustrated by Peter Harrison

From time to time we are faced with something that demands that we should act quickly — but not in panic. Too often when people are faced with the unusual they rush off and do the wrong things — because they haven't stopped for a few seconds to think.

Here are six emergencies — things that could happen in everyday life while you are around. Would you know what to do?

Look at each picture carefully for a minute and make up your mind how you would react. Then write down — in order — the things that you would do.

There are few 'right' answers — for each situation will be slightly different and what suits one, might not necessarily be 'right' for another similar (but different) incident.

If you turn to page 60 you can compare your 'answers' with ours. When you've tried these 'emergencies' on yourself, take the book to Troop Night and see how the rest of your Patrol make out — and how their 'answers' differ from yours and ours. It could be very interesting!

(1) Car crash! You are cycling along a country lane with another Scout from your Patrol. As you turn the bend in the road, you see a car on the far side of the road. It has hit a tree. The driver is slumped over the wheel and the passenger is in the road. What do you do?

(2) **Accident! You are in the Group stores with the rest of your Patrol, packing tentage away after a weekend camp. Another Scout trips over a tent that's on the ground. As he falls, he catches his arm on a bread knife and the blade cuts his arm badly. The wound is bleeding heavily and he feels faint. What would you do?**

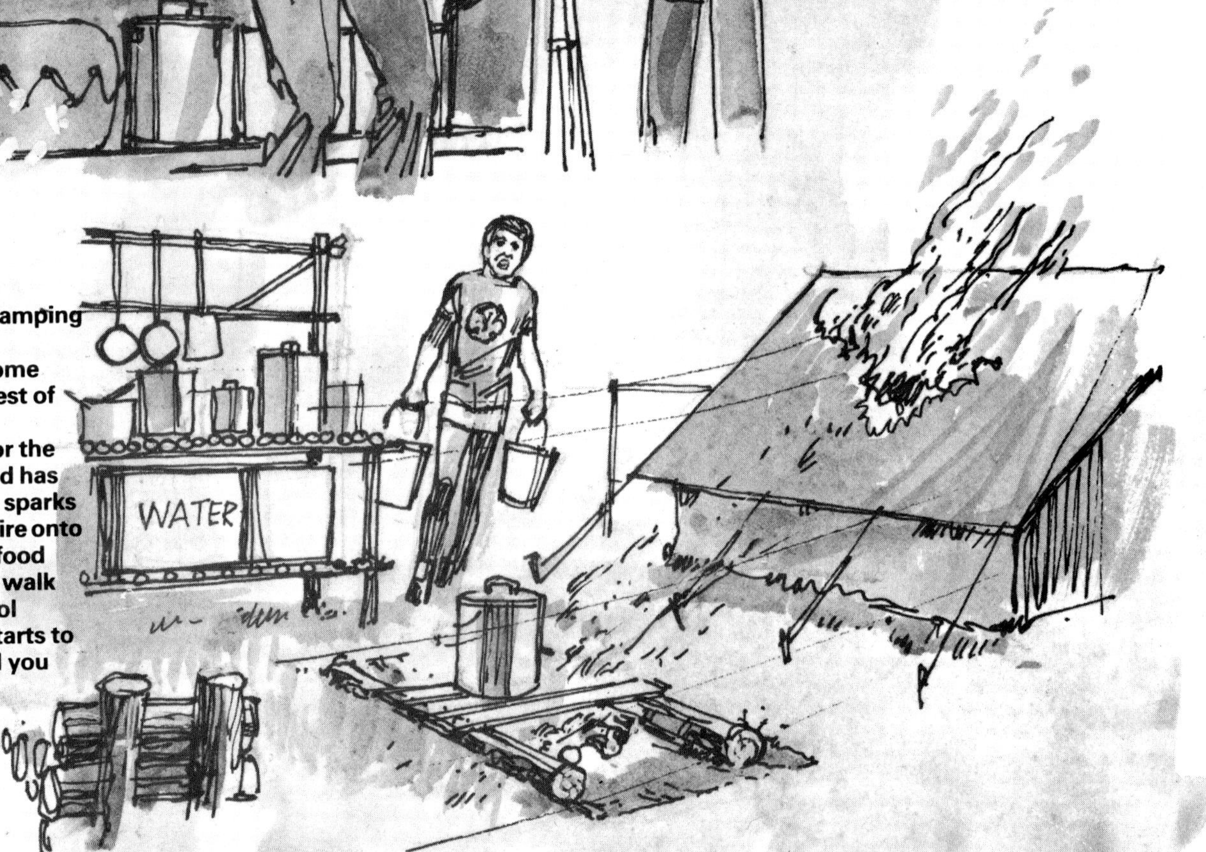

(3) **Fire! You are camping with your Patrol. You've been for some water, while the rest of the Patrol are out collecting wood for the fire. A sudden wind has come up, blowing sparks from the cooking fire onto the canvas of the food store tent. As you walk back into the Patrol kitchen the tent starts to burn. What would you do?**

(4) **Help! You are walking on the towpath by a river when you spot a younger boy leaning over the water from the bank, trying to catch a stick that's floating past. He topples forward and falls in. His cry for help makes you realise that he can't swim — and he's being swept downstream in the current. What do you do?**

(5) Break-in! You are on your way home from school, walking past a friend's house. You know that the family is away from home for a few days and you notice a man climbing through a ground floor window. What do you do?

(6) Danger! You are crossing a footbridge over a railway track. Looking down you see two boys clambering down the embankment towards the lines, carrying a piece of heavy timber between them. What do you do?

Well, what would you do? When you've thought each emergency through, turn to page 60 and compare your solutions with ours.

"One day perhaps I'll play here!" Spencer Davies stands alone in the vastness of Southend United's football ground — and gets the chance to learn better football from the professionals at a Football Association . . .

SOCCER SUMMER SCHOOL

Written and photographed by Denys J. Branch

If you want to learn to play the piano you go to a music teacher and for driving a car you'd go to a driving school or find an expert to teach you. But some things are different and you are expected to become proficient just by picking up skills in a hit and miss way. Football is often like that — once you've learned the rules, you are expected to be able to play a reasonable game without any real training.

Spencer Davies, of the 2nd Hadleigh Scout Troop, plays football at school and for the youth team of a large club near where he lives — Hadleigh Town.

It was to help the footballers-of-tomorrow like Spencer that the Football Association, the game's governing body, set up a number of training schools in different parts of the country. Spencer went to a summer soccer school based on Southend United's ground to learn a bit more about the game and its rules and skills.

When these summer schools started a year or so ago they were an experiment. If they were successful, they would be repeated in other parts of the country. Successful they were — and more and more are now being held. There could be one near your home . . .

Why a summer school?

You've probably seen advertisements for football training schools in newspapers and you may wonder why the Football Association needs to set up its own.

A spokesman for the FA told us: "Many of these so-called schools of football charge more than £50 for a day's training. They're not all like that — but some are — and you merely kick a ball about and have a talk with an ex-player or team manager who is not employed by a Football League side. Perhaps you get a few autographs, but little else."

Starting in the summer of 1982, the Football Association's training schemes are based on League Clubs and last a week. Everyone who is accepted receives a playing shirt with the England badge and the words 'F.A. Soccer School' on it, plus a football.

There's training in ball skills, fitness and so on. During the week there are competitions and finally a series of games to be played and enjoyed.

And in 1982 all this cost £12.50!

Lucky!

Spencer was lucky. His local professional team is Third Division Southend United and when the news went around that there was to be a football summer school there were many more applicants than the 120 places available — and Spencer was one of the lucky ones!

Training started on Monday morning at ten — sharp! And after a short lunch break, the day finished at four in the afternoon.

After explaining what would happen throughout the week, Terry Mowle, the Course Director, split the boys into groups of twenty, each trained by qualified instructors, all players for Southend United. Spencer was in a group led by Frankie Banks, the Club's Youth Coach.

For the first half-hour no one touched a football. "If you start kicking a ball without a warm-up period," said Frankie, "you could strain yourself badly and not be able to play. We'll start gently with exercises each day and they'll get a little harder as the week goes by!"

Spencer Davies — a Scout in the 2nd Hadleigh — was one of 120 youngsters at Southend United's soccer summer school.

Sometimes it was just fun with a ball — but always to obtain perfection with ball control.

Spencer — wearing his shirt with the England badge — takes in points from Terry Mowle, the Course Director.

Skills need practice

Following the warm-up came ball training. Each player had his own football and was encouraged to practise dribbling and shooting.

"The ball must become part of you," Frankie told them. "You must use every spare moment playing with it so that it becomes second nature to beat your opponent or to shoot whenever you have the opportunity."

First he showed them how to kick the ball from a stationary position and then as it rolled along the ground. Later they learned how to trap the ball as it came through the air or how to kick it while it was still in the air.

They were told to try each move and then to try it again — until it was perfect every time.

As the week continued, the training became more and more difficult. There was no let up — and one young man who tried to be a nuisance and clearly wasn't interested in the course was soon on his way home!

Competitions were held, with penalty-kicking and ball-heading, and over the last two days there were football games on a knockout basis.

Throughout the week Southend United's Manager had been looking in and making notes and on Friday afternoon he presented them all with Certificates to show that they had taken part in the Southend United Football Club's Young Players Coaching Course. Awards were made to those who had won the various competitions and — perhaps most important of all — the coaches reported on those in their teams who had done particularly well.

Successful

Terry Mowle summed up the week. "Without doubt, it's been successful. Everyone has learned a great deal about the game and a few have shown that they have the ability to go a long way in football."

Before every session Frankie Banks, the Club's Youth Coach and leader of Spencer's group for the week, gave them limbering-up exercises designed to stretch every muscle in the body.

"Get your head over the ball!" shouts Frankie Banks as Spencer takes his turn to volley the ball at the net.

Dave Smith, the Manager of Southend United, invited some of those taking part to attend further training with the Club — he thought that at least two of them might be good enough to become professionals in a few years' time.

If you're interested in football — and would like to take part in a similar summer school — find out if there's one near your home. Your games teacher or club coach should be able to tell you what's available locally.

At the end of a hard week a Certificate that cannot be bought, but has to be earned.

Looking for some new equipment? Dave Budgen offers some practical advice when you ask . . .

WHAT SHALL I BUY?

Camping and walking are two things that always seem to go together. Most of us seem to begin by going camping and then going out for walks from our camp. Many will then later move on to go walking and carrying their camping kit on their backs — so finding a far greater freedom to roam and explore.

Once we start going out walking, whether it be on country paths or out on open moors, most of us gradually become more ambitious in our ideas — and therefore in our needs too. The 'welly boots' and plastic 'mac' that were quite good enough for the ramble around the local paths and woodlands no longer seem so adequate when our route takes us over high or rough ground. It is at this point that we should be asking — "What kit do I *really* need?", "How much will it cost?", "How do I find out what to look for when buying?"

The basic needs for a walk in our variable climate, whatever the time of year, are simple — a waterproof jacket, warm trousers, at least one thick jumper, stout footwear, something to carry spare kit and sandwiches, and a compass (you'll *always* need a compass if you are using a map of any kind).

Most of you can probably find or improvise many of these, at least to begin with (do take care with trousers though — *cotton* trousers such as 'jeans' or 'cords' are very unsafe once wet). Don't just look in your own cupboards; one of my Venture Scouts once found a good strong pair of woollen trousers in a Group jumble sale — and paid 10p!

In the next pages we take a look at some of the things that are harder to improvise as the walks become more adventurous. For the Scout who likes to walk and enjoys camping some of them are also things that he is likely to want to buy sooner or later — so for each item there is a list of the points to look for (or avoid) when buying — to help in making a choice.

Background photographs by Dave Siddons
Photographs of equipment supplied by Scout Shops Limited

Trento boots, from Berghaus. The tread shown is the 'vibram' pattern. Note also the use of hooks and 'D'-rings.

On your feet — boots

Though we no longer think that only large heavy boots are right for walking, the following are still points to look for when choosing your footwear:

*A good grip ('vibram' or 'klets' soles);
*As few seams as possible (to reduce the chance of leaks);
*A tongue sewn up to the top of the boot (to keep water out);
*Hooks and 'D' rings for the laces rather than eyelets which will let water get in;
*Some stiffness in the sole and ankle protection for rough ground;
*At least one size too large — you can wear extra socks but can never make a boot bigger;
*Ensure your toes cannot touch the ends to avoid problems when walking downhill.

Find the best you can, but accept that your feet will outgrow them.

Both the traditional-style waterproof jacket with no zip and the very popular zipped-style are shown. Both garments are nylon.

On you — waterproof jacket

A vital item — it keeps water out and stops the wind from chilling you. In exchange you will get damp with sweat — but stay warm. Look for:

*A 'jacket' with zip front rather than a waterproof that pulls on over your head (for ventilation) — zip should be double-ended;
*Most jackets are nylon — and the best waterproof coatings are polyurethane and neoprene;
*No seams at the shoulders;
*Seams should be sealed ('doped');
*Heavy grade nylon (at least '4oz');
*Few pockets — they only let water get in;
*A long jacket so that you sit on the bottom of it;
*A drawcord at the neck that you can fasten — 'friction grips' help;
*A large size for ventilation and to allow room for the odd jumper underneath.

Get the best you can manage.

The 'Type 2' from the Silva range of orienteering compasses. Liquid damped.

With you — a compass

One item that you can't outgrow! An orienteer's compass (the sort with the transparent baseplate) is best, look for:

*Clear markings (in degrees) on the dial;
*Liquid damping of the needle (so it settles quickly);
*Somewhere to attach a long cord (use a spare bootlace) to hang it around your neck, so it is always ready for use;
*Luminous markings for use in the dusk or dark (on night-hikes and those times when you'll be walking the last bit of the journey in the dusk);
*Avoid 'gimmicks' — features you don't really need may make it less suited for walking use.

Remember — you may *really* need this one day, so never go out walking without having it with you — handy too, not in your rucsac!

A Karrimor 'Jaguar'. Typical style of sac used very widely. This one has an internal frame.

Behind you — a rucsac

What a variety of shapes, sizes and colours — and usually features you don't really need, too. Some points:

*Little difference between nylon or cotton sacs;
*Capacity is usually given in litres. For Scouts, 50-55 litres is plenty (adults need 60-65 litres usually);
*No more than two side pockets;
*Two compartments inside may be handier than one:
*A sac with no frame to support it is probably best;
*The 'external' frames used with some rucsacs can be adjusted as you grow;
*Rucsacs with 'internal' frames or stiffening have to be fitted to your back length and are soon outgrown;
*A waist belt helps balancing;
*Avoid top flaps fastened with cords rather than straps as these are difficult to handle with cold, wet fingers.

Keep it simple, look for extras on the next one.

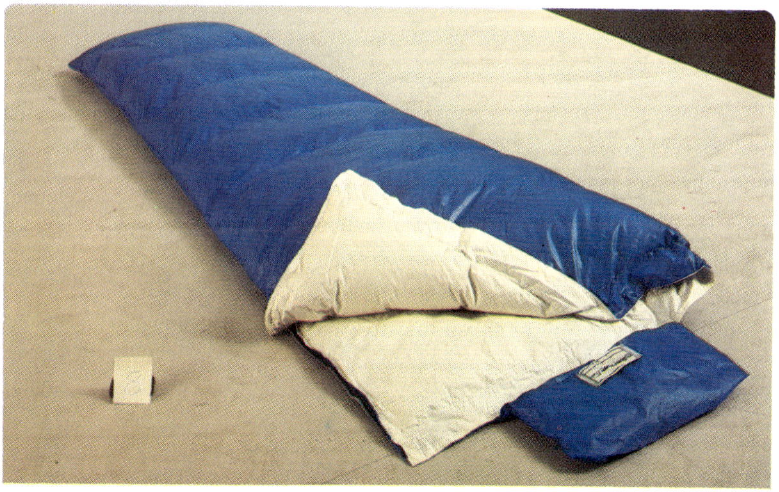

'Blue Moon' from Scout Shops Limited. This is a two-season bag filled with down and feathers. Note quilting and short zip.

Vango Force Ten (Mark 3) — a very popular range of tents in nylon and cotton, with the traditional ridge shape.

Above you — a tent

'Two-skin' tents are best ('inner' tent and 'outer' fly-sheet). Nylon tents are lighter than cotton ones but more 'sweaty'. Look for:

*The best shapes are the simple ridge or one that tapers down to the back;
*'A' poles (two poles in an upside-down 'V') make it easier to get in and out of a small tent;
*A sewn-in groundsheet (essential);
*The fly-sheet should have a 'porch' to protect the tent doors from rain and give space for your kit (there is no room for it in a small tent);
*Zips are the best way of closing tent and fly-sheet doors;
*The fly-sheet should come down to the ground;
*Only a few guys are needed, rubber rings will do the rest;
*You can repair cotton tents yourself.

A Trangia methylated spirits stove. Note that the billy set is packed around the burner when not in use.

Serving you — a camping stove

Camping stoves are *all* dangerous, whatever the fuel, and should *never* be used inside tents. Buying points are:

*Gas cartridge stoves start easily, but are slow and expensive to run;
*Paraffin pressure stoves are messy, but cheap to run and paraffin is widely available (in the UK);
*Meths stoves work well in most conditions, are easy to light and usually include billies in the price. Meths may be hard to obtain sometimes;
*The only 'safe' petrol stove is the 'Coleman Peak 1' — which needs lead-free petrol to run well — otherwise avoid petrol stoves;
*Solid fuel is hard to control but handy for emergency use;
*Cheap, imported stoves may not be a bargain when you need spares.

No 'best answer', but meths is probably the easiest.

Around you — a sleeping bag

Its job is to keep your body's heat in, so buy the best you can. (Note that the better a bag, the smaller it packs down.)

Some points:

*'Natural' fillings (down and feathers) insulate well and pack small;
*Good 'made-made' fillings (eg 'Hollofil') are bulkier packed, but can be washed;
*'Man-made' fillings work better than 'natural' fillings when wet;
*A bag should have no stitching joining the inside and outside as this creates 'cold spots' with no filling between them;
*A tapered or 'barrel' shape is best;
*For warmth have no zip — if a zip *is* chosen, then there should be a strip of insulation behind it;
*Most bags are described as two-season or three-season (the fourth is a Scottish winter). Use a two-season bag from early spring to late autumn.

CAMP FOOD— Glorious Food

Ruth Elliott
photographs by
John Elliott

Many people think that Scouts only know how to cook with a frying pan. We know that Scouts can be good cooks, but sometimes get stuck for new ideas.

Here are a few recipes that you may not know, but first — some important points to remember when planning and cooking meals.

- **Meals should match your activities — you can't swim after a heavy meal, but you'll probably be hungry when you've been swimming.**
- **Everything used in preparing food, especially your hands, must be scrupulously clean.**
- **Results depend on the quality of the ingredients, so always buy the best you can afford.**
- **Plan interesting and varied menus. Have both hot and cold meals; use different ingredients in each meal and vary the method of cooking — boiling, baking, steaming or frying.**
- **Make the meal look appetising. It is tempting to stew meat and vegetables together, but it usually looks uninteresting. Colourful vegetables, separately cooked, add a lot of eye-appeal and encourage the appetite. Salads and cold meals should also be colourful and attractive.**
- **Things take longer to cook outdoors because moving air slightly cools the cooking pots. Different foods take different times to cook, so time each item to ensure that everything is ready just when you want it to be.**
- **Persuade your Patrol Leader to stock basic herbs and spices. Black pepper, bouquets garni, garlic salt, Italian seasoning and thyme each add a distinctive flavour to meat dishes; cinnamon, ginger or mixed spice add flavour to many puddings.**
- **Last, but not least! An attractive meal makes the mouth water, so have enough plates and dishes to present it properly. When someone says: 'Looking at that makes me feel hungry' that's how food ought to be.**

Smoked mackerel paté

Best made the night before you want it.

6 oz fresh smoked mackerel; 3 oz butter; a teaspoonful concentrated tomato purée; freshly ground black pepper; a squeeze of lemon juice.

Discard the bones and skin from fish. Place the flesh in a small basin and beat with a fork until the fish is very finely mashed. Add the tomato purée, the butter, a little black pepper and the lemon juice. Beat all the ingredients together to form a smooth paste, or paté. Butter the inside of a small mould or basin and spoon the paté in, pressing it well down and smoothing the top with a knife. Put to cool, overnight if possible. Run a knife round the mould and turn the paté onto a bed of lettuce. Garnish it with cucumber and serve with buttered brown bread or fingers of toast.

Kipper fillets can be used, instead of mackerel, to give a slightly stronger flavoured dish.

Smoked fish paté would not be a suitable starter if you are having a highly spiced main dish, such as curry. Melon is available at a reasonable price from most greengrocers, and a melon slice also makes a refreshing starter.

Pork chops in a sweet-sour sauce

Four pork chops; a little cooking fat or oil; for the sauce — ½ pt stock, made with chicken stock cube; 8 oz can pineapple pieces; ½ tablespoonful soy sauce; 3 tablespoons vinegar; 1 dessertspoonful tomato purée; rounded teaspoonful sugar; 1 rounded tablespoonful cornflour, mixed to a thin paste with water; 2 large carrots, peeled and grated lengthways.

Heat the oil in a frying pan and brown the chops on both sides. Set chops aside on a plate. Wipe excess fat from the pan with kitchen paper. Put into the pan the stock, juice from the pineapple, soy sauce, vinegar and the tomato purée. Bring the mixture quickly to the boil, stirring all the time. Reduce the heat and dissolve the sugar in the sauce. Still stirring continuously, add the cornflour paste and keep stirring until the sauce has thickened. If you want a thinner sauce, add more chicken stock.

Put the chops into the sauce, which should just cover them. Simmer gently for 15 - 20 minutes. Stir in the pineapple pieces and the grated carrot; simmer for a further 5 - 10 minutes.

Serve with green beans or peas, and buttered noodles.

Chicken marengo — Scout style

Four chicken joints; 2 stock cubes; 2 tablespoonsful cooking oil; 1½ oz butter; flour; 2 onions, peeled and sliced; ½ teaspoonful minced garlic; 4 oz mushrooms, washed and sliced; 15 oz tin tomatoes; ¼ teaspoon each dried marjoram and dried basil; salt and pepper; lemon juice; 4 fl oz dry cider.

Skin the chicken joints and coat them with flour. Heat the oil and butter together in a frying pan, add chicken and fry until joints are browned all over. Remove joints from pan and set aside in a baking dish.

Fry onions and mushrooms together until the onion goes transparent, add minced garlic and cider. Allow to boil for 2 - 3 minutes. Roughly chop the tomatoes and add contents of can to frying pan, together with the dried herbs and a squeeze of lemon juice. Simmer for two minutes, then pour over the chicken joints. Make up the stock cubes, using 1 pint of boiling water, and pour into baking dish until joints are just covered with liquid. Put a lid or foil cover onto the dish and either simmer on low heat, or in a slow oven, 30 - 40 minutes until the chicken is tender. Correct the seasoning if necessary.

Serve with freshly boiled rice.

All-year-round salads

Salads can be eaten all year round, so there is no special list of ingredients. Make use of vegetables as they become available. Some fruits — such as pineapple chunks or orange or grapefruit segments — are tasty and colourful in salads, and mix well with the more usual salad vegetables.

Apple slices need to soak a few minutes in salted water to prevent them turning brown. Chopped walnuts or roasted peanuts are a crunchy contrast to cottage or cream cheese. Red or green peppers may seem expensive, but a quarter of a large pepper finely sliced would be sufficient for a large mixed salad.

When you have chosen your salad fruits and vegetables prepare them according to type — wash, peel, grate or slice. Arrange the main salad attractively on a large serving plate. Mix some smaller continental-style, one-vegetable or two-vegetable salads with a vinaigrette dressing.

Make the dressing by putting the following into a screwtop jar and shaking it to blend them — 1 tablespoonful olive oil; 1½ tablespoonsful vinegar; ½ teaspoonful dry mustard; sprinkle of black pepper.

Experiment with things you may not have tried before — you'll be surprised how varied and interesting salads can be.

Ginger pudding

4 oz each of caster sugar, margarine and self-raising flour; two size 3 eggs; 2 teaspoonsful ground ginger; 5 pieces preserved ginger, chopped coarsely.

Beat together the caster sugar and margarine until pale and creamy. Break eggs into a cup and beat them lightly; gradually beat eggs into creamed mixture. Add the ground ginger, chopped ginger, and 1 tablespoonful of flour and beat again until spices are absorbed. Use a metal spoon to fold in the remaining flour, a little at a time to avoid forming lumps.

Grease a 2 pint pudding basin and put a circle of greased greaseproof paper in the base. Put the pudding into the basin — it should come about halfway up. Put greased greaseproof paper and a cloth, or foil, cover over the basin. Tie the cover round the basin and make a string handle across the top. Stand the pudding in a large pan containing enough boiling water to come two-thirds way up the side of the basin. Boil gently for 2½ - 3 hours, topping up with more boiling water as needed.

Serve with custard, ginger sauce, or ice-cream.

Raspberry mousse

Two 1-pint raspberry jellies; one 14½ oz can of evaporated milk; ½ lb fresh or frozen raspberries.

Stand the can of evaporated milk to chill for several hours in really cold water.

Boil a measured ½ pint of water, remove pan from heat and dissolve both jellies in it. Pour into a measuring jug, add cold water to make just under one pint. Put into a cool place until nearly set.

Mash the raspberries until they form a fine purée.

Whisk the chilled evaporated milk in a mixing bowl until it is frothy and almost doubled in volume. Do the same in another basin with the nearly-set jelly, then beat in the raspberry purée. Whisk the jelly and raspberry mixture into the evaporated milk.

Rinse a mould, or individual moulds, with cold water and pour mousse into the dampened mould. Cover with foil and leave standing in cold water until needed.

Unmould onto serving plate and decorate with fresh or tinned raspberries. Serve with ice-cream, chocolate sauce or real cream for a special occasion. This is enough for six servings — or four plus seconds! Other soft fruits can be used with suitably flavoured jellies.

YOUTH HOSTELLING in Derbyshire

John and Ruth Elliott

Six Scouts, two Venture Scouts and a Leader set out to follow the route which John Merrill, the famous explorer, named the 'Limey Walk'. A large area of Derbyshire consists of limestone which has worn into the lovely, deep dales and high hills.

They started at Ashbourne . . .

. . .and walked to Dovedale, where they crossed the famous stepping stones. They stopped occasionally to look at some of the fantastic limestone caves, and had lunch sitting by the riverside.

Overnight accommodation was booked in Youth Hostels, which are numerous in the Peak District, so it was easy to plan comfortable daily walking distances between Hostels.

Most hostellers cook their own supper and breakfast and . . .

Alan Gordon, Editor of SCOUTING, meets a famous former Scout who today works in the world of television as we follow . . .

A day in the life of – Michael Hurll

Michael Hurll is an Executive Producer with the BBC. In his Scouting days he was Stage Manager of Ralph Reader's famous *London Gang Show*. Today he is responsible for BBC Television's pop music output. Some of his shows include *Top of the Pops The Late, Late Breakfast Show* (with Noel Edmunds) and *The Two Ronnies* (with Ronnie Corbett – himself a former Scout – and Ronnie Barker).

Michael Hurll, former Scout who learned stagecraft with the *London Gang Show* and now Executive Producer of BBC TV's *Top of the Pops*.

Michael Hurll told Alan Gordon . . .

"I normally like to arrive at the Television Centre well before eight in the morning. My working days vary a lot, but there is a pattern to the week.

"Wednesday is *Top of the Pops* day and at 8.30am I go to the studio to make sure that everything is ready. We do have problems from time to time. At the moment there's an electricians' strike and we are having to pull out all the stops to ensure that the Christmas Show will go ahead. Normally, everything is in good shape and I go back to my office to work on some other of my productions.

"Rehearsals start at eleven in the morning. Each pop group is rehearsed by me to ensure that camera angles are right and to sort out any problems there might be – such as groups wanting their work interpreted in a certain way. We work out costumes and all this keeps us busy until about six in the evening. The audience arrives at 7.30pm and we record the show. This is normally over by about nine – and the rest of the day is my own!

"Life for me can be really hectic as I am totally responsible for *Top of the Pops*. I decide what goes in it, I look after the budget and I decide the running order. I have to do all this within thirty-six hours!

"The new pop charts arrive at nine on Tuesday morning. We will only allow groups whose records are going *up* the charts to appear on the show, so we cannot put a running order together until Tuesday morning – only twenty-four hours before rehearsals are due to begin.

"We also insist that no record can appear on the show for two consecutive weeks and I also have to decide whether the record – or, indeed, the performers – are suitable for television.

"As I have said, *Top of the Pops* is only one of my productions. I also produce *The Late, Late Breakfast Show* and I will never forget the week when ABBA appeared live. I had to go over to Stockholm on the Monday to line up the interview, on Tuesday and Wednesday I came back to London to work on *Top of the Pops*. On Thursday and Friday I was putting the final touches to *The Late, Late Breakfast Show* and on Saturday

. . .here you see a typical Youth Hostel kitchen, but you have to be early to find it this empty. Everyone made his own bed — with Skip making sure they did it properly!
Up early to cook breakfast and do a share of the hostel chores, and away by ten in the morning for another day by tumbling rivers and along winding dale paths towards . . .

BBC Radio One disc jockeys – Peter Powell, John Peel and Tommy Vance.

A view across the studio floor as Bucks Fizz rehearse.

The mass of cables and cameras that the viewer does not see – with Spandau Ballet rehearsing.

evening it went out live. And, just for good measure, we spent the evenings of that week rehearsing and recording the autumn series of *The Two Ronnies*. Thankfully, not all weeks are as hectic as that.

"We had a lot of headaches with *The Late, Late Breakfast Show* when it first came out. However, we overcame these and it became a great success with the public. The spinning wheel, where viewers could be selected at random to do daring feats, is very popular in America, but we were the first British Show to use the idea. We decided we would keep it for adults as children have *Jim'll Fix-it* and there was nothing that was exclusively for grown-ups. The 'People's Chart' is the hard work of Hellen Fielding who came to us from John Craven's *Newsround*. All in all, I lead a very busy life, but it's great fun.

"I don't have much time for relaxation but when I do I like to participate with my two sons who are avid sportsmen. One plays rugby for London Welsh and I like to go along to watch him. I am also a keen Queen's Park Rangers Football Club Fan and I watch whenever I can. During Wimbledon Fortnight we virtually live at the All-England Club and I like to help out with the local Scout fête whenever I can.

"I enjoyed my days in the Cubs and Scouts immensely and I was proud to be the Stage Manager of the *London Gang Show* in the 1950s – what exciting days those were! I am only sorry that I cannot take part in a team game, but with my commitments to work I would probably have to cry off games a lot and I would not like to have to continually let my team-mates down.

"I am often asked by young people what advice I would give them about a career in television. 'How does one break into television work?' they ask. The answer is that it is very difficult. Television is going through a recession these days. When I was a young producer, I made a few mistakes. These days we can't afford to make mistakes. All this makes life difficult for the inexperienced person wanting his big breakthrough.

"However, nowadays we want technicians. We are on the look-out for cameramen, for video tape operators and for people with technical knowledge. If you have your heart set on being a 'front man' then get experience with the local dramatic society and then try to break into local radio."

Photographs by Julian Simmonds

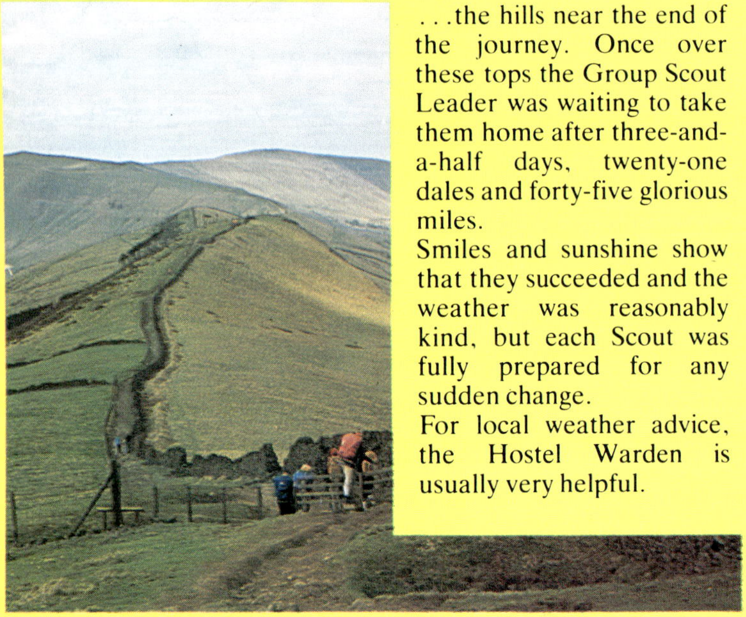

. . .the hills near the end of the journey. Once over these tops the Group Scout Leader was waiting to take them home after three-and-a-half days, twenty-one dales and forty-five glorious miles.

Smiles and sunshine show that they succeeded and the weather was reasonably kind, but each Scout was fully prepared for any sudden change.

For local weather advice, the Hostel Warden is usually very helpful.

If your Scout Leader joins the Youth Hostels Association, he can have a group Introductory Pass. Providing that no members of the party have been hostelling before, the pass-holder may take fifteen Scouts for three consecutive nights in Hostels. After that, each individual would need to join the YHA, but the annual subscription is low and there are about three hundred Hostels to choose from in England and Wales alone. Scotland and Northern Ireland have their own Youth Hostels Associations.

History doesn't have to be boring and the best way to start enjoying it is to go out — and find history for yourself!

History in the street

Written and photographed by Bill Bruce

How well do you know the place where you live? As a Scout, you probably know it well enough to direct strangers and to take useful short-cuts, but how much do you know about the history of the place?

Look along any street and you'll see all sorts of things: lamp posts, notices, signs, bollards, coal-hole covers, fire hydrants, pillar boxes, memorials and so on. Nearly all these items have a story to tell and finding them in the first place can be quite a challenge.

Obvious

The most obvious pieces of 'street furniture' are the roadsigns themselves, but there are very few old ones left these days. Until 1858 the only signs on the road were milestones and posts, but when heavy steam engines began to move about, many landowners put up signs warning of low bridges and weight limits. Most of these early signs were made of cast iron and a surprising number have survived. At the end of the last century, a cycling craze swept across the country and some cycle clubs put up signs to warn riders of steep hills and other hazards. The very first 'steep hill' notice was put up at the top of Muswell Hill in North London. Most of these old signs have now gone, but you will sometimes find an odd one or two tucked away almost out of sight.

Old street name signs survive all over the country, often side by side with their modern replacements. Some are enamelled with white letters on blue or green backgrounds while others are cast in lead or iron.

Look out for reminders of the last world war; you may still find Air Raid Precaution (ARP) signs on the sides of old houses.

If you can spot them, many old houses carry the date when they were built. Nearly all public buildings, chapels and so on also show their own history. Make a list of the dates and find the buildings that were built around the same time — it could point to a period of great prosperity in the town.

Common

Surprisingly, a fairly common sight on old houses are fire marks. In the eighteenth century, insurance companies covered properties against fire — and also ran their own fire brigades.

It's understandable that the firemen employed by the insurance companies would only deal with a blaze if the house that was burning was covered by the right company — so each insurance company had its own firemark and displayed it on the walls of the buildings it insured.

Take a look at the lamp posts on the street. Most of them will be modern steel or concrete posts, but there are still quite a few old ones around. The first street lighting Act was passed through Parliament as long ago as 1671, but the oldest lamps that you will find in use date from the early nineteenth century. They are mostly ornamental and usually made of cast iron.

This building used to be called 'Waterloo House' and the name can still be seen in the faded paintwork above the doorway. It is now a shop, but has it always been? The local reference library could help you to find out.

You can tell at a glance that this pillar box was erected during the reign of George V. Check the dates on the houses nearby and you may be able to put an exact date on the whole street!

Pillar boxes can give a good guide as to when a street was built as they always bear the initials of the reigning monarch.

Surprised!

Look down as you walk around the town — and you may be surprised at what you see!

In the past, everyone used coal or wood to heat their homes and to cook their meals — and many streets with older houses still have coal holes dotted along the pavements, although most are now disused.

All the coalman had to do in those days was to lift the cover and pour the coal straight into the cellar, thereby avoiding tramping dirty coal dust into the house.

Many of these covers were very ornamental and have the name and address of the foundry where they were cast — and sometimes the date, too.

Look out for plaques telling where famous people lived and why buildings and memorials were erected. Statues and benches often have inscriptions and commemorate all sorts of events and people.

Find it!

Make a survey of all that you can find and try to build up a picture of the history of the place where you live. Keep a record of your finds — take photographs, or better still, make brass rubbings and sketches.

Visit the local library and compare what you have found with old maps of the place and books about its history. There may be a local history society that would be only too pleased to answer any questions — and you may discover something that they've missed!

There's history in the street — if you can find it!

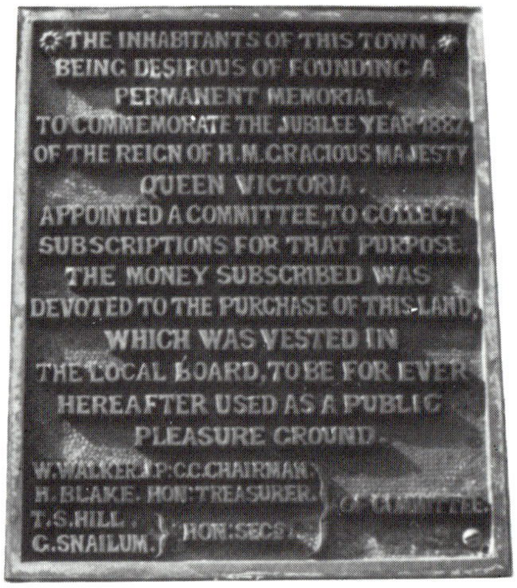

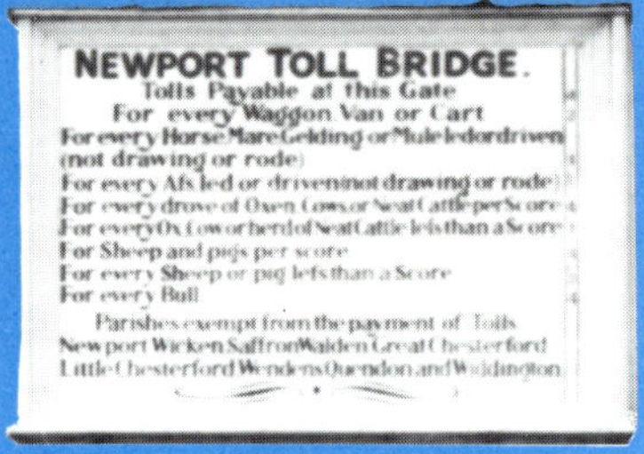

Plaques can tell a complete story and reveal information about people, dates and places. Others — like the toll bridge sign — remind us of a very different way of life.

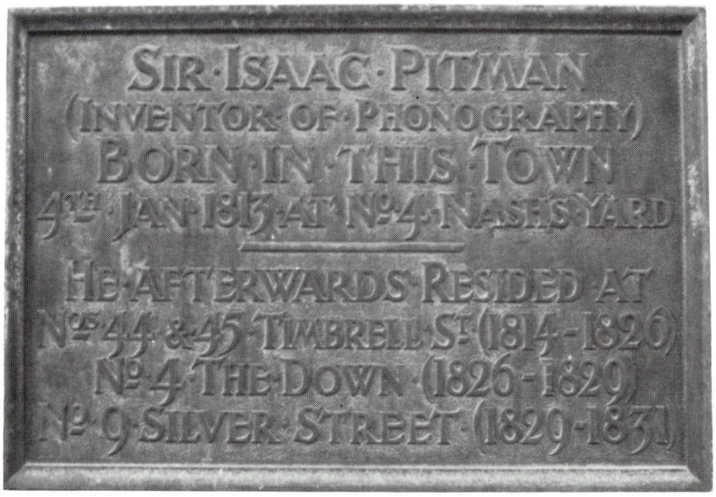

Here's a recent commemorative plaque set into a London pavement. Things don't have to be very old to be 'history' and signs that are being put up today will be 'history in the street' in but a few years' time . . .

David Saint provides some light relief with . . .

A Knotty Problem!

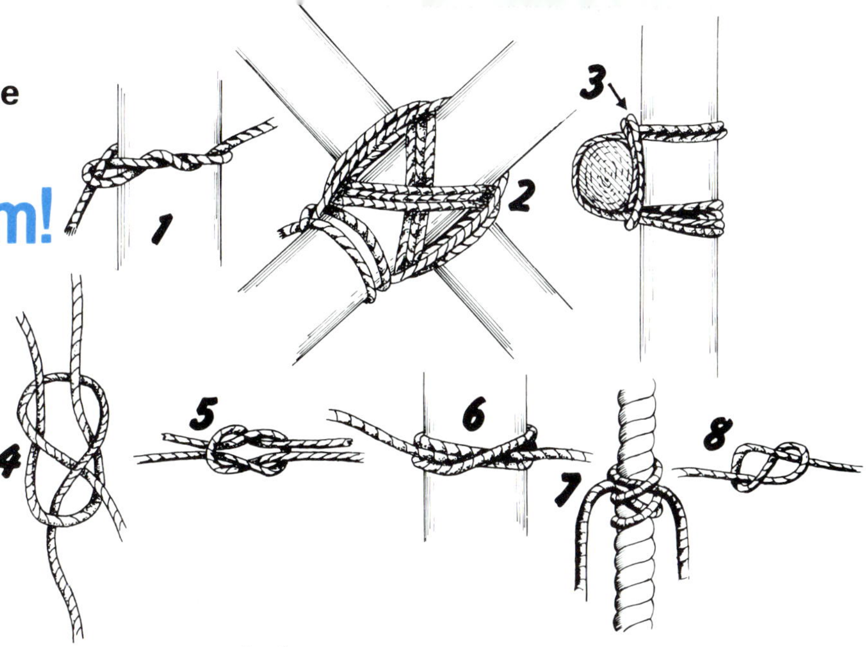

Illustrations by Bill Bruce

The illustrations will help to solve the eight anagrams — and you'll need to know some pioneering terms, too!

The name of the town you spell out has a place in the history of the Scouts.

Anagrams

(1) Thimberchit
(2) Allongia shading
(3) Punfring trap
(4) Dense beth
(5) Not freek
(6) Citch hovel
(7) Chilli throng
(8) The fig or figue

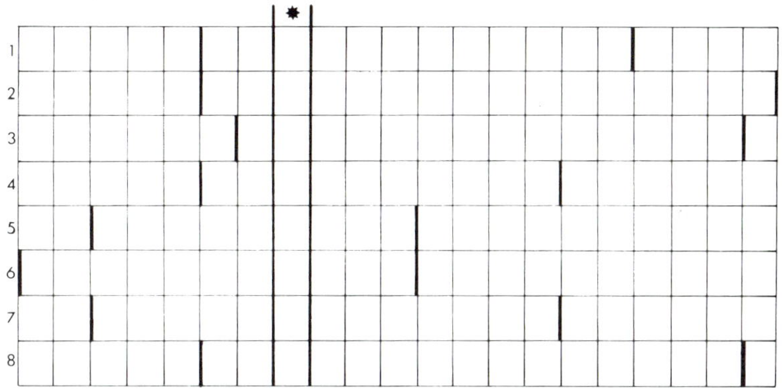

Answers on page 61.

Patrol Leader Chris Crevier passes the Pyramids on his way to . . .

Troop Night~Egyptian~style

I'm a Patrol Leader in Cairo, Egypt — in the British International School Scout Troop. Our Troop Nights are a little different out here. To start with, we meet in the afternoons from two-thirty onwards. My route to Scout Meetings is certainly different, for I have to pass the Great Pyramids at Giza, those monuments to the Ancient Egyptians.

I often spot tourists gazing in awe at these last remaining wonders of the ancient world, but I sometimes find it difficult to stifle a yawn, so familiar is the sight!

Our uniform is a nice mixture of Egyptian and British. We wear grey trousers, a fawn Egyptian shirt, British badges and finish it off with a Scout green scarf. We started by wearing T-shirts, which was fine in the hot summer, but the winters out here are surprisingly cold.

My Patrol reflects the international make-up of the Troop for I have Scouts from Canada, India and New Zealand as well as Great Britain — and I'm from the United States of America. There are some twenty nationalities represented in the Troop, but it's very friendly and we find that new Scouts settle in very quickly.

Our progress scheme is the same as in Britain. I've recently gained my Advanced Scout Standard, but because it's difficult to do some of the things in the requirements, our Scout Leader has to bend the rules a little from time to time.

My favourite camp site is on a citrus farm and our main activity there has been the construction of a hut — from mud bricks. If we are directing new Scouts to the camp site we tell them to 'take the first right at Cheops Pyramid and keep going straight on!'

Pitching a tent on sand isn't easy — as you'll find out if you try for yourself!

Chris Crevier, Patrol Leader of the Panthers, strides out on his way to Troop Night — in the shadow of the Great Pyramids at Giza.

Photograph: Ian Jones

KIELDER The Dam

Written and illustrated by Bill Bruce

In the heart of one of Europe's largest man-made forests is one of the biggest man-made lakes — KIELDER WATER — over 185,000 million litres of water held back by the enormous KIELDER DAM . . .

The earth embankment of the dam is just over one kilometre long and at 52 metres, it stands as tall as Nelson's Column in London. It has a volume of over four million cubic metres and took four and a half years to build.

Over 1 million trees were felled in the 125,000 acre Kielder Forest, and homesteads and farms were evacuated to make way for the reservoir.

Flooding the area took two winters and the project was officially opened early in the summer of 1982.

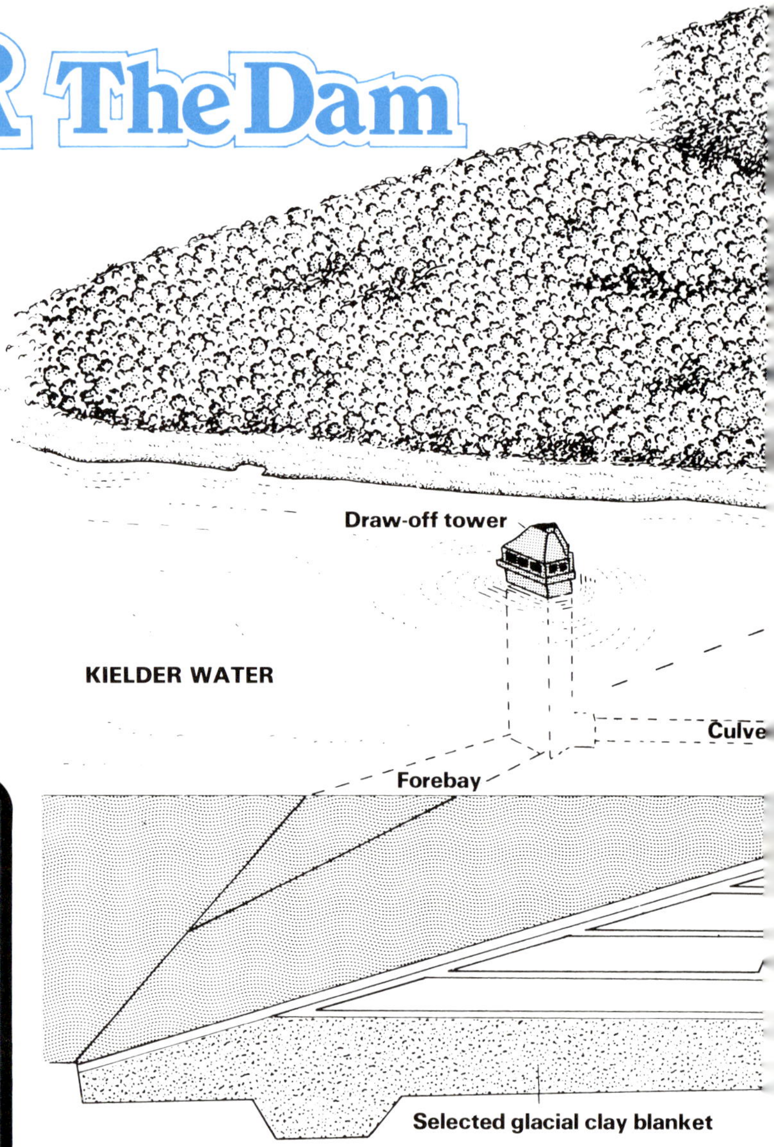

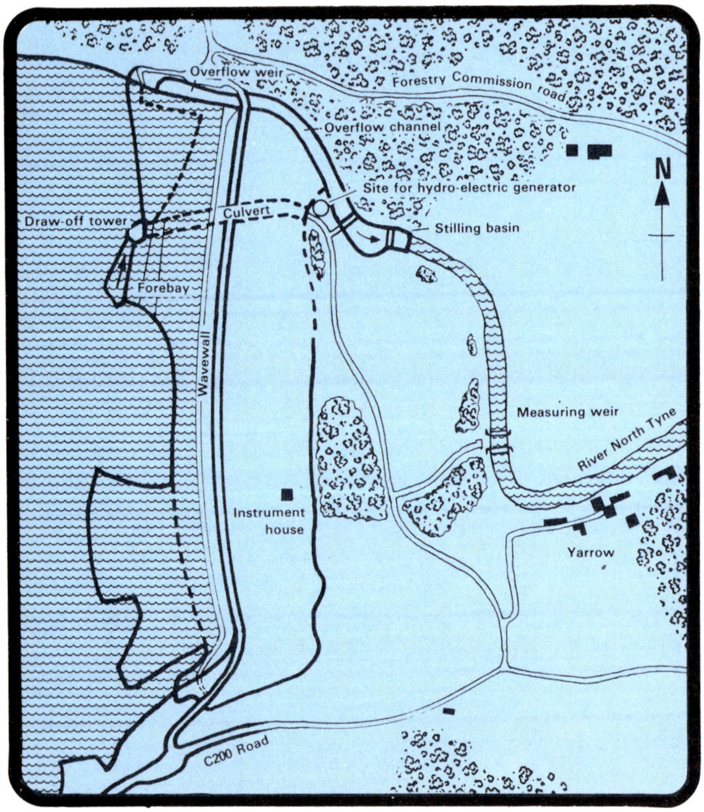

A plan of the Kielder Dam site

The Kielder Water Scheme has been designed to meet all the expected demands for water in the North East of England well into the 21st century.

Provision has also been made to install hydro-electric generators at Kielder Dam to make use of relatively cheap hydro-electricity, sufficient to power 100,000 sixty-watt lightbulbs or a town with a population of up to 10,000.

To the north-west of Kielder Water is a flat, shallow area and when the water level is low, unsightly mud flats would be seen, so a secondary dam in the form of a weir has been built at Bakethin. The top of this small dam will usually be under the surface, until water begins to be drawn off in large quantities at Kielder Dam.

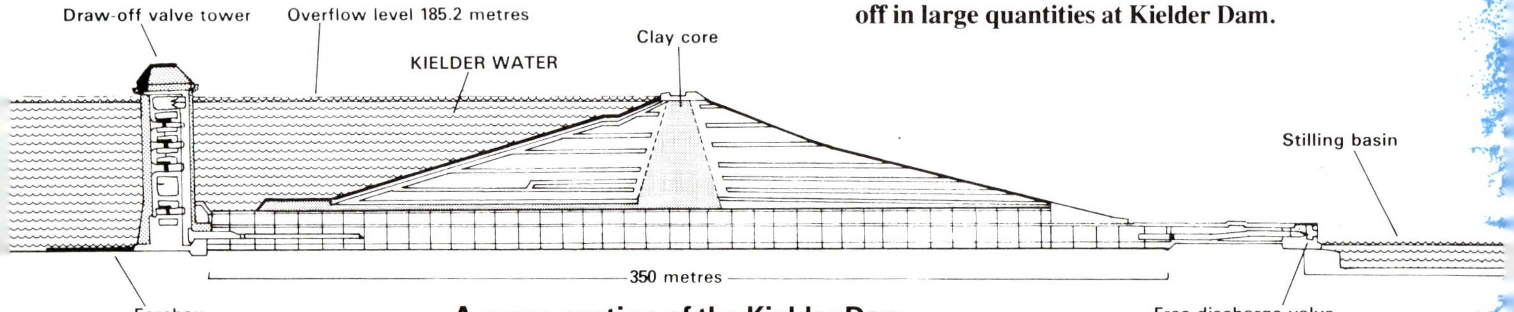

A cross-section of the Kielder Dam

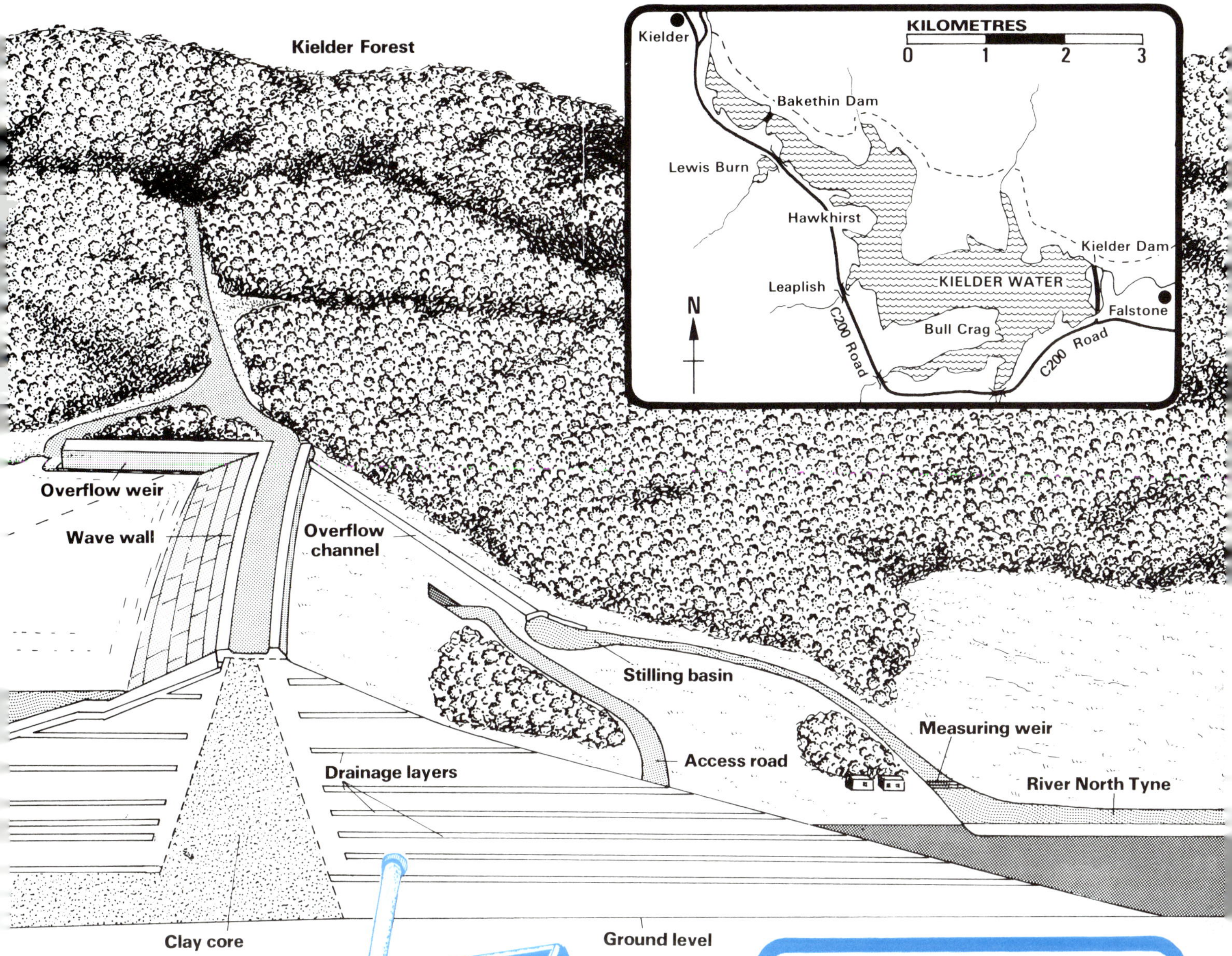

Water released from the Kielder Dam will flow 58 kilometres down the rivers North Tyne and Tyne to Riding Mill. From there, the water can be transferred through a pumping station which is the largest in the country, and taken through long underground tunnels to the rivers Wear and Tees.

Some Kielder facts and figures . . .

Kielder Dam
* Length: 1,140 metres
* Height: 52 metres
* Volume: 4.1 million cubic metres
* Overflow level: 185.2 metres
* Maximum flood level: 188 metres
* Valve tower height: 70 metres

Kielder Water
* Length: 12 kilometres
* Surface area: 1,086 hectares
* Capacity: 187,980 million litres

Bakethin Dam
* Length: 165 metres
* Height: 12.5 metres

Tunnels
* Total length: 32 kilometres

It has been estimated that one in every four men in the United Kingdom was a Scout at sometime. On this page — and later in the Annual — Geoff Platt meets three young men who decided to try something different. First, Chris Wright explains . . .

I'm in the Air Training Corps because...

Chris is a member of the 1066 (Hitchin) Squadron Air Training Corps (I know that's right as I was given a piece of paper with the Squadron's full title written on it. Like the Scouts, the ATC want you to get the name correct!). Chris was fourteen when we met and he used to be a Scout, but didn't like it because they didn't do anything and the Leaders didn't seem to bother . . . so he decided to try something else.

Two of his friends were in the local ATC Squadron, so he went along with them and has been going ever since.

Chris Wright, a member of the Air Training Corps in Hitchin.

Chris says that the activities are varied and he never gets bored. He plays the bugle in the band and enjoys taking part in carnivals, fêtes and the Remembrance Sunday Parade in November each year. He has been parascending, hiking and mountaineering, full bore and .22 shooting, flying in Chipmunks and gliders, and camping and on night exercises. The Squadron camps each year on an RAF base.

Meetings of the Squadron are held on Mondays and Thursdays, with band practice on Sundays. On Mondays they have lectures and project training – aircraft recognition, modelling, motor transport, signalling, demonstration drill and so on. On Thursdays there are personal projects and sports.

The ATC have a progressive training programme like the Scouts – First Class Cadet, Leading Cadet, Senior Cadet and Staff Cadet. And there are ranks, too: in the 1066 Squadron they have a Flight Sergeant, three Sergeants and four Corporals.

The Squadron finds time to raise money for others. During the Wings Appeal for ex-servicemen they collected £1,400 – not bad for a week's effort.

Chris obviously enjoys being an Air Cadet. It has made him think about the possibility of joining the RAF when he's older.

In fact, Chris enjoys it so much that he forgot to tell me about the Squadron's big weekend activity when they act as marshals at the Flying Association's International Rally. For a weekend in July they keep the aircraft in the air and the cars on the ground – with a little help from their friends and other Squadrons!

Ron Jeffries suggests some activities — a few of which may be new to you — to try . . .

Now that you're a Scout

Whether you were a Cub Scout in the Pack or came direct in the Scout Troop, you must have had some ideas about the sort of activities Scouts enjoy. You expect Scouts to go camping and hiking, to cook their own meals, practise first aid, take to the water in canoes and dinghies; but there are lots of other things, too.

Very often it's the unexpected and the unusual activities that you'll enjoy most — sometimes as part of that camping, hiking, cooking, first aid or whatever. On these pages we are showing some of the things that Scouts do — a few may be well-known to you, but others might just spark off an idea that will give you and your Patrol some fun next time you are out together . . .

Comfort

We spotted these Scouts on their Patrol site under the trees at Broadstone Warren National Scout Camp — with a table that made eating comfortable (and was ideal for writing that letter home, too!). Timber found on the ground was lashed to make the table top, with legs at one end and a convenient tree trunk at the other for support. Logs were dragged up as seats. Simple — but effective!

Pioneer

Knots and lashings have to be practised and perfected, but the best place to do so is in the outdoors with spars and ropes – making something that's fun for the whole Patrol. This tower was constructed completely by young Scouts at an International Jamboree in Ireland. If there were language problems amongst the different nationalities, they clearly knew how to tie a lashing firmly.

Just a pallet

On many a camp site the wood-pile is a treasure-trove for the Scout who likes to improvise. At Tolmers National Scout Camp Site when we were there wooden pallets were all the rage — and here's a Scout using one as a raft! After a while they tend to become water-logged – and there's the danger of sinking – but often the air trapped under the pallet will keep it afloat long enough for an afternoon's fun in the warm sunshine.

Just the chance . . .

Your Troop might enjoy canoeing (or some other water activity), but there are Scouts who would give anything for just the chance to get into a boat and enjoy the thrills of the water. Our photograph shows a Scout who spends all his daylight hours in a wheelchair — and it was other Scouts who gave him 'the chance' he'd been waiting for. Find out if there are Scouts living near your home or when you are away camping — Scouts who have a handicap that prevents them doing all the things that you enjoy. With your Patrol Leaders, and Scouters' help, they could have 'the chance'. Well, couldn't they?

Winter jogging

There are activities to suit most seasons of the year — and when the snow is thick on the ground, keeping warm is sometimes not merely an activity, but a vital necessity, too! Jogging in your nearest park helps you to do just that — and to enjoy the beauty of the snow at the same time. Find another Scout in the Troop who would like to jog regularly each day, before or after school perhaps. Start off with short distances and work up to longer ones as you get used to running (or, rather, as your muscles get accustomed to the exercise!).

Stop the rot!

Tents are expensive and one way to extend the life of a Patrol tent that's served your Troop well is to give it a re-proof when it needs it.
These Scouts have erected one of their Patrol tents at their local camp site on a dry day and are brushing on the proofing liquid that will keep the rain out at summer camp. If you and your Patrol have not proofed a tent before, have a word with the Group's Quartermaster to see if he would like you to lend a hand when the weather is right and there are maintenance jobs to be done.

Circular eggs!

When you fry eggs in camp — either in a frying pan or on an improvised hot-plate as here — it's difficult to keep them from spreading all over the place and running into each other. Here's a Scouter who's found the answer! Before camp he cut rings from a length of metal pipe and each egg was broken into its own individual 'cooker'. Great — on hamburgers or fried bread!

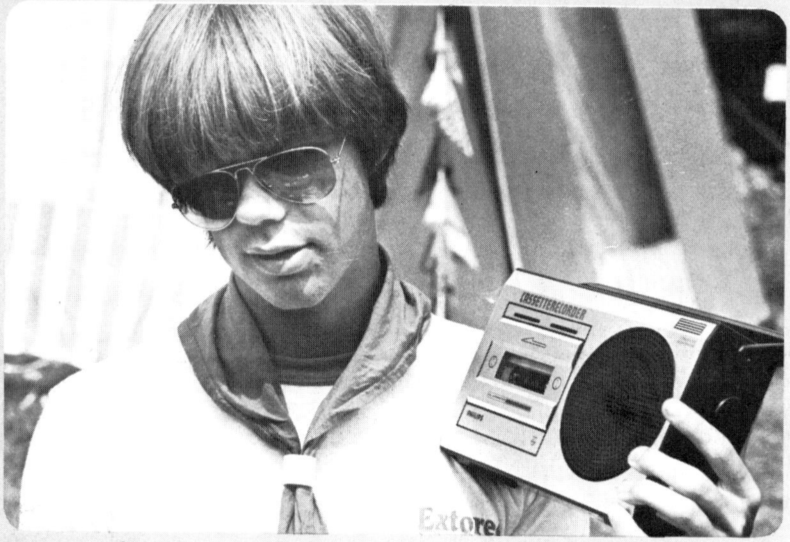

Listen

Just as an experiment, suggest to your Patrol Leader that part of one Troop Meeting is run with everyone blindfolded. For a short time it will be fun, but there's a more serious side to this, for when the laughter dies away, think what it would be like to be blind all the time. This young Scout from Denmark was camping at Extoree in 1982, the international camp when Scouts with handicaps worked and played side by side with other Scouts so that both could enjoy a wide range of activities. Most of the Scouts could read the camp's daily newspaper, but Bue Vester-Andersen was able to listen to a taped version on a portable cassette recorder, for he has been blind from birth. Up and down the country there are 'Talking Newspaper' groups — volunteers who tape local newspapers and magazines for the blind and partially-sighted in their home town. The Redbridge Talking Newspaper Group taped Extoree's daily newspaper for the blind. Find out if there's a 'Talking Newspaper' group near where you live. Ask if you can visit them to see what they do.

Photographs by Bill Bruce, Ron Jeffries and Julian Simmonds

Alan Gordon, Editor of SCOUTING, meets another famous former Scout — now the manager of Fulham Football Club — as we follow . . .

A day in the life of– Malcolm Macdonald

Malcolm Macdonald, the manager of successful Fulham, was a Patrol Leader in the 15th Chelsea. Before entering management, he had a brilliant career as a player, including international honours for England. Malcolm Macdonald holds the record as the English player who scored the most goals in a single international football match – five against Cyprus.

Malcolm Macdonald told Alan Gordon . . .

Malcolm Macdonald talks with two local Chelsea Scouts on Fulham's Ground. Paul Lacey (left) is a keen Fulham supporter, but Peter Benn (right) admitted to the fact that he follows Manchester City!

"I usually leave home at seven in the morning and like to arrive at Craven Cottage, our West London ground, before nine. This gives me the chance to organise the rest of the day before setting off to our Roehampton Training Ground in South-West London.

"Training starts at 10.30 each morning when the coaches and I put the players through their paces. We could be working on new tactics, discussing our match performances and we usually pit our first team against the reserve and apprentice players in a training match.

"We train until one when we have lunch. Our chairman invariably joins us for lunch and that gives us the chance to discuss club matters before I go back to Craven Cottage to deal with administration.

"There is always a huge postbag which demands a lot of attention and I like to hold a daily staff meeting with my coaches and youth development officers where problems can be discussed and sorted out.

"Naturally on match days my programme is different. On Saturdays I leave home at nine in the morning and my first job is to watch the youth team in action. Their matches kick off at eleven and, come the final whistle, I dash off to Craven Cottage for the big game. I hold a staff meeting at one and then head for the dressing room at 1.45pm.

"Another little job is my weekly column in the *Daily Mirror*. This usually involves two or three meetings a week where I discuss my ideas with a reporter from the newspaper and then jot down my thoughts.

"Soccer is a great game and I am continually being asked what I would advise a youngster who wants to become a professional. My advice is simple. Practice! Work hard at your game – it's the only way – and, in particular, pay attention to the art of the 'one touch'. First-time passing of the ball is vital.

"I enjoy my job. I am finding football management very satisfying after a happy playing career."

Photograph by Ted Gatt

Out overnight or away for the weekend?
Dave Siddons shows you how to . . .

Build a Bivouac!

It's great fun to build yourself a shelter and to sleep in it overnight. Usually the best place to build one is in camp — as you'll need permission from the landowner and the right materials to build it with.

There are many different ways of constructing a shelter from natural materials, but there's one golden rule if you want to keep dry . . . make sure that the roof has a steep slope. Flat-roofed bivouacs just don't work!

The photographs on these pages show how to construct a shelter which is triangular in shape and big enough to sleep two Scouts.

The roof is of ordinary bracken, but reeds, large flat leaves or even moss are equally effective if you can get them.

Whatever materials you use, ask permission first. You will need some poles for the main structure, so look for timber that is dead and not alive. If you have to cut live timber, make sure the landowner gives his permission and do this neatly.

Remove all trace of your shelter at the end of your camp and leave the timber tidily for someone else to use after you.

First, you need a long, stout pole to act as the main roof support. Rest this in the fork of a tree about one and a half metres from the ground. Make sure that the ground around the tree is comfortable to lie on! Bracken or grass under your groundsheet will make a softer bed.

Next lay thinner branches against the pole and secure them with creepers or even with thin, flexible twigs.

Tie the lashings firmly — and don't cheat by using string!

You'll need to weave a large number of thin, flexible twigs in and out horizontally to form a firm base for the roof covering.

Put your roof covering on from the bottom upwards, making sure that each layer overlaps the one below it — like slates on the roof of a house. You'll need lots and lots of bracken for this: just imagine what it might be like inside if you get a thunderstorm or hailstones lashing down!

It's a good idea to dig a trench around the outside of your shelter to stop the rain running off the roof and then inside. With the shelter completed, you just need a groundsheet and sleeping bag — and you're set for the night!

You can make the task of keeping dry easier if you build your shelter under a tall tree with thick foliage. It won't be subjected to direct rainfall — just to drips from the tree!

All ready for the night — and a dry one!

You can make a shelter that's much more watertight using polythene sheeting. If natural materials are not readily available (or if the landowner prefers you not to use them) this can be the answer — but it's hardly what we'd call a 'backwoods' shelter! Lash two poles together at the top, spread out the feet — and then rest a stout pole between them and the tree.

Spread the large sheet of polythene over the 'ridge'.

Pull the sides out and hold them down firmly with stones or large logs. We couldn't find any stones or logs large enough — but there were some bricks handy and they will do just as well.

Just the job — if you don't mind sleeping in a see-through tent!

Shoot for GOLD

John and Ruth Elliott

If you want to make a start in archery, find out where your nearest archery club is by asking at your local library, citizens' advice bureau or information centre. Or you could write to the Grand National Archery Society, c/o NAC, Stoneleigh, Warwickshire.

Archery is a skilful sport and it's important to learn from a qualified instructor.

The Scouts in these pictures were lucky enough to find a club which ran a beginners' course for them. The course fee included the hire of all necessary equipment. First of all they had to help put up the 4-foot targets, and Michael is setting up the ground quiver and bowstand to hold the arrows and bow when not shooting. The target here is 20 yards from the shooting line. The instructor made sure that everyone knew some important safety rules — never point a loaded bow at anyone, and wait until everybody has finished shooting before dashing forward to check your score!

Heavy Horse Scouts

Written and photographed by Michael Edwards

There are few sights that illustrate the quiet charm of the English countryside better than a pair of Shire horses straining at the plough. Thirty or so years ago the heavy Shires gave way to today's highly mechanised farming, but there are still some farmers who rely on horse-power.

Henry Mee, of Bretherton, a village in Lancashire, is one, and a stroll around his 50-acre farm of ploughed fields and growing crops could make you think you are living in another age — before the machines took over.

The 1st Longton Scout Troop has paid a number of seasonal visits to Henry Mee's farm and the Scouts have seen for themselves that there's still room for horses.

Scouts John Maddocks and Geoffrey Bullock set off for the field they are to help plough — with two magnificent Shire horses, two tons of power and muscle.

With the Shires hitched to the plough, Henry Mee shows John and Geoffrey how the blades will cut into the soil.

"It's simply a matter of keeping the plough straight," Henry Mee told the Scouts. Easier said than done, as the Scouts found they had muscles in places they did not realise before!

Rupert is being helped to hold his bow in the correct shooting position, still without an arrow. If he hadn't learned this properly then the arrows could well have just flopped at his feet when he started shooting. Andrew has mastered the correct shooting position, and his instructor is showing him how to use one eye to sight along the arrow to the target. Although all the Scouts shown here are right-handed, bows are available for left-handed archers. Notice that everyone is wearing an armguard and finger tabs — so that forearms and fingers don't get sore from the bowstring.

It was a cold February morning and as the horses' breath condensed in the air, the Scouts realised just how chilly it was.

Later Henry Mee was ready to drill the cereal seed for a later summer crop in the ground ploughed by the Scouts — and here he fills the seed hopper.

Back in the stables, Ian Prescott feeds one of the Shires.

Henry Mee drills the cereal crop — sown in the spring it will be harvested in late summer and, again, the Shires provide the muscle-power.

Alan Walker holds aloft one of the Shire's collars — leather-made and stuffed with straw for comfort

Three or six arrows are shot by each archer and two or more may shoot from the same stand. The round is not finished until every archer in the shooting line has shot all his arrows. Then — the fun of adding up your first score, removing your arrows from the target and getting ready to shoot again!

After only four weeks one Scout took the Bronze Medal in a Beginners' Competition, and they all hope eventually to gain the Master-at-Arms Badge.

They've had a great time — and we're sure that you would enjoy getting started in archery.

Philip Watts tells Geoff Platt . . .

I'm in the Boys' Brigade because...

Founded in 1883 by William Smith in Glasgow, the Boys' Brigade is older than the Scouts. William Smith was a friend of Lord Baden-Powell, the Scouts' Founder.

William Smith was concerned about youngsters in Glasgow who roamed the streets with nothing to do. He organised a club – similar to a Sunday School – and the organisation grew from there. Today there are Boys' Brigade Companies in thirty-five countries throughout the world and the movement has just celebrated its centenary.

Philip Watts is thirteen and a member of the 1st Letchworth Boys' Brigade Company. He has been a member for five years and joined with a friend. He liked the games and was impressed with the Christian approach and commitment.

The Company is divided into Squads, with a Sergeant and Corporal in charge. The leaders are called Officers and there are six running the 1st Letchworth.

Meetings are held on Wednesday evenings. There's inspection and drill – sometimes in preparation for a competition – training classes in things like first aid and communications for one of the Brigade's training badges, some football or gymnastics.

Philip has been canoeing, is a side-drummer in the band (playing at carnivals, festivals and fêtes, traction engine rallies and church services).

On Sundays Philip attends Bible class, when an aspect of life is studied and discussed, and then related to teachings in the Bible.

Philip feels that the Boys' Brigade has given him a very good knowledge of the Bible, with plenty of fun and enjoyment through the Company's activities.

Philip Watts, side-drummer with the 1st Letchworth Boys' Brigade Company

Tess Pickford journeys through jungle and by dug-out canoe with Scouts going to their . . .

Troop Night ~ Solomon Islands ~ style

The lagoon is usually free of sharks, but now and again one slips through the barrier reef, which makes it advisable not to dip a cut finger over the side of the canoe into the limpid waters, for sharks are soon attracted by blood.

That's the sort of danger that a mother warns her Scout son about as he pushes his dug-out canoe down the village beach to paddle his way to Troop Night in the big village, three bays along the island. Or he may have to go further, across the sound to the next island, shimmering in the glare of the tropical sun. It's a bit different from getting on your bike in Glasgow or Manchester — and having mum call after you to watch the traffic as you pedal your way to Troop Night!

But we're in the Solomon Islands, a small Commonwealth country composed of hundreds of islands stretched across a thousand miles of sea. Getting to the nearest Troop Meeting can be an adventure in itself!

For some Scouts it will mean a five mile trek through the bush and along a trail which can disappear in a day under a tangle of creepers growing hourly in the humid heat. He'll need his bush knife to clear a way for himself. Around him flash birds of vivid colour, while huge insects scowl at the human intruder, their raspings only stilled by the crash of a coconut from the heights above!

But a greater hazard comes in fording the rivers — for a sudden storm in the mountains can bring a flash-flood within minutes. Solomon Island Scouts are well aware of the dangers and take no chances. They wade quickly across the shallow water just before the tropical storm breaks and the rain comes streaming like a waterfall onto their bare backs — for they trek to Troop Night not only with bare feet, but carefully carrying their shirts and scarves.

For a Solomon Island Scout's journey may be rough, but when it's time for flag break he's smart in the pride of his uniform.

'Crab football' is much the same the world over, but for these Solomon Island Scouts the adventure of getting to Troop Night can involve jungle-trek or dug-out canoe.

A Scout Patrol camping on one of the hundreds of islands in the Solomons.

KIELDER The Place

Written and illustrated by Bill Bruce

The Kielder Water project was designed primarily to provide water for the industrial North East, but it has also created a unique environment for wildlife and an exciting new area for all sorts of leisure activities.

Surrounded by the huge Kielder Forest, Kielder Water provides new opportunities for boating, sailing and trout fishing.

The area around Bakethin Dam has been set aside as a nature reserve and interesting nature trails run along the wild north side of the lake. The native forest wildlife has remained relatively unchanged since the lake was created, but now many other wild animals and birds have begun to thrive in the area. A few of them are illustrated here.

Before the lake was flooded, many archaeological sites — some dating back over 2,000 years — were excavated and other historic features were protected, such as the 120-year-old Kielder Viaduct which was once part of the North Tyne Railway and which crosses the lake at its northern end. Kielder Castle dates from 1775 and now serves as the local headquarters of the Forestry Commission.

There is a major Scout Adventure Camp at Hawkhirst in an area ideal for everything from backpacking and pony-trekking to orienteering and canoeing.

All this makes Kielder a place that's well worth a visit . . .

A map showing the position of Britain's largest man-made lake. For a detailed plan of the Dam and its surroundings, see pages 20 and 21.

On pages 20 and 21 there is a feature on the building of the Dam that has helped to create this unique area of countryside . . .

ANIMAL Weather-Forecasters

Written and illustrated by Anthony Wootton

It's a fact that animals' senses are often considerably more acute than ours. A dog's sense of smell — as you will know if you have a pet of your own — is far superior to man's, while a hawk can see its prey from a much greater distance and more clearly than we could ever hope to do.

These things apart, it often seems that animals have an *extra* sense, in addition to those of smell, taste, touch, sight and hearing — a 'sixth sense', which is much less easy to define or describe.

Take animals and the weather. Country people will tell you that many kinds of animals actually know in advance if it's going to be fair or foul. Not only that, but they will insist that observation of birds and beasts (both wild and domestic) can give us humans a more reliable guide to what's going to happen to the weather than anything the much-criticised meteorological office can come up with!

It would be nice if it were true, but unfortunately such claims tend to be more than a little exaggerated. Animals can no more tell the future than we can. Certainly any long-range weather forecasts based on their behaviour are likely to be just as unreliable as those from the weatherman on TV (through no fault of his own, I would add, for Britain's climate is subject to so many constantly changing influences).

Sharper

Nevertheless, since animals tend to be sharper on the sensory uptake than we are, they are able to pick up 'nature's signals' just that little bit quicker and act accordingly — if not always in the way that we might expect!

Rooks are an interesting example of this. When they fly up to a considerable height and then plummet straight down again as if they've been shot (and they often are!) repeating both movements several times, then rough winds and stormy weather are likely to be on the way.

Just why rooks behave like this (and it's called 'break-necking' in my part of Buckinghamshire) is uncertain, but as animals are not above playing, it's possible that they are simply enjoying themselves. They're probably taking advantage of the variable air currents that are around at the appoach of a storm. Whether or not they seek shelter immediately after their bit of sport, I can't say!

The height at which birds fly is often a guide to the weather. When starlings fly high it can indicate fine, settled weather.

Belief

Other rook weather lore simply doesn't stand up to close examination. There's an old belief that if rooks make their nests in the topmost branches the following summer will be a fine one. If they build lower down the tree, we'll be in for strong winds and storms that are likely to bring their homes crashing to the ground if they went higher.

It's unfortunate for tradition that anyone who watches rooks regularly will know that they tend to use the same nests year after year (perhaps with a bit of patching up here and there) whatever the weather turns out to be!

A more reliable meteorological guide is linked to the height at which birds fly. Swallows, swifts and martins often soar to a great height in fine settled weather. In those conditions the upper atmosphere is a living larder of insects attracted upwards by the sunlight and the columns of warm air (thermals) rising from the sun-heated earth.

As soon as the birds begin to take a lower flight path, a change for the worse can be expected, for reduced pressure and winds disperse the insects over a wider — and lower — area.

When birds — such as these house martins — seek a lower flight path, bad weather can be expected.

Cattle commonly use hedges and trees as wind-breaks and this may indicate worse weather to come.

It is sometimes possible to tell the temperature from crickets' rate of chirpings. This is a female oak bus-cricket (*Meconema thalassinum*). Females don't sing!

Farm animals

Much traditional animal weather lore concerns farm animals, simply because they were more regularly observed in the past than wild creatures.

Cattle tend to use hedges and large trees as shelters and windbreaks and when they huddle together it *may* indicate that worse weather is to follow. Mostly, however, they are simply doing what we would in similar circumstances — trying to shelter from what's happening at the moment rather than what might come along shortly!

Sometimes you'll notice that cattle appear restless — and are not just lazily grazing or lying about. This could mean that there's a storm on the way, particularly if the animals make sudden dashes across the fields, for in thundery, humid weather horse-flies or gad-flies are at their most active, stabbing cattle and people alike!

Insects

Insects have long been quoted in connection with the weather. Certain black beetles, more especially the common violet ground-beetle (*Carabus violaceus*), are called 'rain-beetles' in some areas — and if you see them (or step on them) it's said to herald rain. Once again, however, this is usually linked to conditions at the moment rather than in the future, for beetles tend to emerge from their lairs after rain to search for worms and other small creatures which become more active in wet weather.

Crickets are among the more interesting weather forecasters (although weather 'indicators' might be a more appropriate word). Like many other insects, crickets are most active on warm, 'close' evenings and seem to chirp more loudly and merrily as the temperature increases.

It is said that you can tell the temperature from a cricket's rate of chirping! Penguin Books published a paperback in 1943 called *The Weather*, where the authors tell us that if you count the number of chirps made by a cricket in fourteen seconds and add 40 to this figure, the result will be the current temperature to within just a few degress Fahrenheit!

Other researchers have come up with similar ideas, but using different formulae. I've not tried it for myself, largely because even the common house-cricket (*Acheta domesticus*) is getting increasingly difficult to find. But many years ago, when I lived in a very old cottage, we had a cricket in the stonework near to the open fire — and that one was certainly more lively with his chirps when we had a good blaze going in the hearth.

Spiders

Spiders are not insects, of course, but they too have weather-links — if not very reliable ones. When a spider re-builds or strengthens its web, it doesn't suggest (as some people maintain) that the strength of the web is about to be tested by high winds. Most spiders do some web re-building every day as a matter of course and it has little or nothing to do with the weather.

On the other hand, if you see or are tickled by strands of gossamer (the silk exuded by young spiders which helps their dispersal) this may suggest settled conditions because warm, dry weather helps the process of non-violent spread.

Most spiders re-build or at least repair their webs every day. This is the web of a species of zygiella, common in gardens and near houses.

The common garden cross spider (*Araneus diadematus*) in web.

Truth, half-truth and . . .

Much animal weather lore is a mixture of truth, half-truth and absolute nonsense! It's a vast subject and books in the library will give you many more examples.

Better still, talk with older country people when you are away at camp or on a hike. Their lore will vary from place to place and it's a fascinating study!

When you've collected some more examples of animal weather lore, see if they work and, if they do, pass them on to other Scouts.

The violet ground-beetle (*Carabus violaceus*) often emerges at night during and after rain — and they are called 'rain beetles' in many parts of the country.

A camp fire is a great way to end the day. Dave Siddons shows you how to make one — safely.

Camp fire's burning!

'What's the happiest part of camp life?
It's when the night has just begun,
Round a jolly camp fire, when a hard day's work is done.
It's darkening! The cold comes and settles for the night,
And it's much too dark for reading, and bedtime's just in sight.
So you get your friendly blanket and you twist it round your back,
And squat beside the dancing flames and hear the hiss and crack . . .'

Those words were written by a 13-year-old Scout nearly thirty years ago — but they're just as true today! You can bet your life that whenever someone lights a fire at camp — especially if darkness is coming on — then it will attract Scouts like a magnet!

There's no better way of rounding off a day at a Patrol camp than to build a camp fire and for the Patrol to gather round it as darkness closes in.

Here's how to build a camp fire properly — and safely — for your Patrol to enjoy at their next camp together.

First find a suitable spot — away from trees which could catch fire, but sheltered from the wind. A woodland clearing or a corner of a field will do fine. Carefully remove a one metre square of turf. Take the turf to a shaded, cool place under trees and store it there. Keep it watered until you are ready to put the turf back into place again. Poke a long stick into the ground in the middle of the square and carefully make a pyramid of very thin, dry twigs around it. Hawthorn is best, but it's essential that you use plenty of it.

Continue building the pyramid, but use slightly larger twigs (about the thickness of your finger). You will find that you will need a lot of wood at this stage. Leave a hole on the side nearest the wind: this is where the fire will be lit.

Make sure you have permission to light fires. It is essential to do this before you choose a camp site, as you will need fires for cooking.

The next step is to cut some large logs. These, too, must be of dead, dry wood. Hawthorn, ash, oak and pine are ideal. Two of these logs are placed on the ground — one on either side of the pyramid. The next two are placed across these on the other sides — and so on to make a sort of tower around the pyramid.

As the tower gets higher, cut the logs to shorter lengths so that it slopes inwards. The theory is that as the top logs burn through, they will fall into the centre of the fire and keep it going.

Never use paraffin or other inflammable liquids to help to start your fire. Apart from the very real danger of getting yourself burned in the sudden *whoosh* of flame, it doesn't actually help very much in any case — and it simply shows you up as incompetent. Any fool can light a pile of paraffin-soaked wood, but it takes a good Scout to light a fire properly.

Finally, find some good thick logs (that are preferably wet) and place them around the base of the fire. These will protect the grass from the heat. Don't be tempted to throw these logs onto the fire later — they are there to stop the fire spreading onto the grass.

Just before the fire is to be lit, push some crumpled paper into the centre on the side nearest to the wind. Dry grass or bracken will do just as well if you can find some.

There are various ingenious ways of lighting the fire, but a safe and effective method is to make a torch. This is simply a long stick with sheets of newspaper, cardboard or even straw bound around the end. The torch is lit with due ceremony and — when it's burning well — it is thrust dramatically into the base of the fire on the side nearest the wind.

In no time at all your fire will be burning merrily and — in the words of the Scout-poet . . .

'There's life, there's joy,
there's happiness,
there's friendship
and there's fun,
All a-singing round the
camp fire when the day's
work is done.'

At the end of your camp, remember to clear up the ashes and either bury them or dispose of them as the landowner requires. Water the ground well and then carefully replace the turf when the soil is cold. Fill in the cracks between the pieces of turf with earth and try to leave the spot exactly as you found it.

Alan Gordon, Editor of SCOUTING, meets another famous former Scout — and hands over the interviewing to two of today's Scouts — as we follow . . .

A day in the life of – John Craven

The well-known BBC Television programme *John Craven's Newsround* has been entertaining and informing young people for more than ten years. We asked two Scouts, Ali Catterall (13) and Paul Rymer (12), of the 15th Chelsea Scout Troup, to turn the tables and interview the man who has, over the years, interviewed thousands.

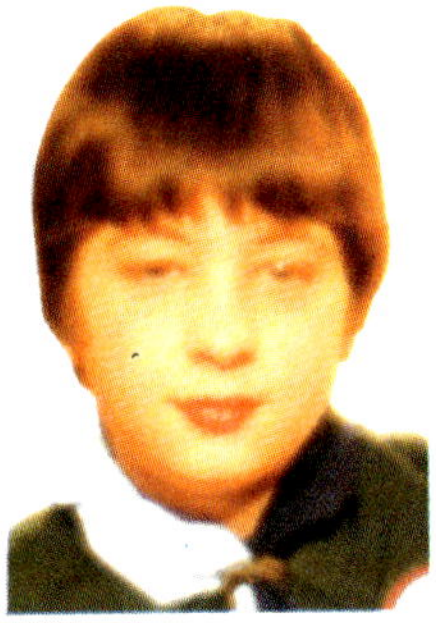

Ali and Paul in the *Newsround* studio with John Craven.

Ali: *'Have you ever been in the Scouts?'*

John Craven: 'Yes, I was in the 17th North-West Leeds Scout Troop. I joined the Cubs at the age of eight and I became a Sixer.

'In the Scouts, I was the Patrol Leader of the Wolf Patrol and I still keep in contact with some of the many friends I made in the Movement. One such friend is in Australia, where he is a geologist, and we still write to each other.

'What I enjoyed most was getting out of the big city and going camping. I loved the climbing and caving. It really gave me a great sense of adventure and a sense of purpose, especially when I was a Patrol Leader and I had the responsibility of five other people.'

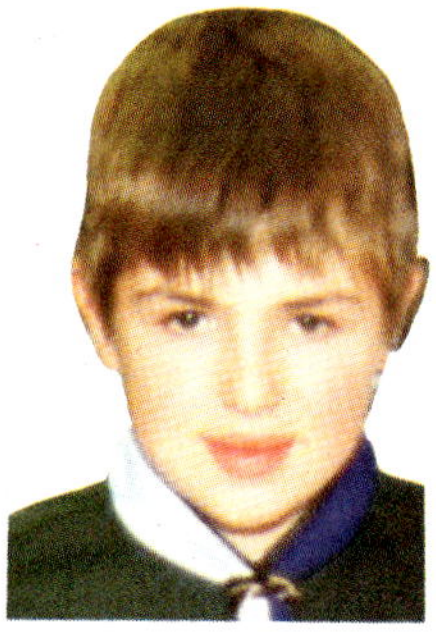

Paul: *'What's a typical day for you?'*

John Craven: 'We have a morning *NEWSROUND* meeting at around 10.15 am and I arrive in the office a few minutes before it starts. We have six people working on the programme and someone has already read through the newspapers. We each read a couple of newspapers as well, and we get together and talk about the stories that we have read or we know are about to happen during the day.

'It is here that we decide the rough outline of the programme and the stories we might be using that evening.

'During the morning we do our research, such as finding film or video tape or getting more information about the stories. At 2 pm we have another meeting in which we decide the final format of the programme and draw up what is called a running order.

'This has all the details of every story, the length of each story, the order it takes in the programme. The length of a programme can vary between six minutes and nine. There is a lot of work going into a short programme. For example, on the programme that went out just before you came to the studio to do the interview, there were three of us working on three stories with me writing the script for one.

'By about 4.30 pm there is a meeting down in the studio with the programme's director, the camera crews, sound engineers and others involved in the programme – such as the people in charge of the photographs, charts and maps. We go through the running order, decide how everything is going to go and which camera is going to take pictures of what in the studio. If they get a chance, they rehearse the films and the video tapes, just to make sure everything is alright.

'I get to the studio at 4.50 pm, the make-up girl puts a bit of powder on my nose, I comb my

Paul takes over and sits in John Craven's seat – is this the start of a new programme *Rymer round*?

hair and then we're on the air at 5 pm!

'It's quite a lot of effort, as you can see from all that, to do six minutes or so of television.'

Ali: *'What is the most important programme you have ever worked on?'*

John Craven: Oh, that's a difficult one! Obviously *NEWSROUND* is very important to me. I've been doing the programme for ten years. I started it and it is very much part of my life.'

Ali: *'What are your plans and proposals for the future?'*

John Craven: 'I don't have a lot of plans! I don't really plan things! I've been very lucky, things have always happened to me without me having to make any plans.

'For six years I was involved with *Swap Shop* and I had a lot of fun there. As a newsreader you are quite a serious person and on *Swap Shop* I had the chance to be a bit more human. I became involved in the new programme which replaced *Swap Shop – Saturday Superstore* – and I have done a lot of things for them.

'I have recently finished a series of programmes called *The Show-me Show* which I found fascinating as it was all about science, but we tried to make it into interesting, fun science and I hope everyone understood it.

'I like everything I do. I'm very lucky in that I get a choice of things to do.'

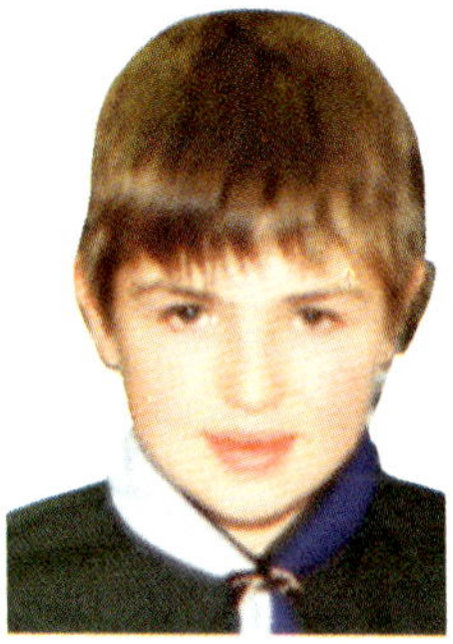

Paul: *'What has been the worst thing to happen to you on a programme?'*

John Craven: 'There have been quite a few disasters in the 1,500 *NEWSROUNDS* over 10 years. The other week, the main film never arrived on the screen. I tried three times to get it but, due to a mistake in communications, we showed the headline film three times. Eventually I had to admit defeat!

'On one other occasion I was telling the viewers all about an African elephant but, for some strange reason, the film was about a Japanese supermarket.

'I have an earpiece and I listen to what goes on in the gallery. The gallery is the place where the producer, engineer and all the people connected with the programme sit and I hear all their conversations in my ear. I also hear the sound effects of the films.

'We had the story about Abdul, the oldest elephant in Africa, and he had just died. We had some library film of Abdul. I read the introduction to the film. These introductions are all on my autocue machine which is like a roll of toilet paper which goes round in front of the camera with the words on it. The words for the film or video tape, however, are all on a hand held script.

'I heard in my earpiece the sound of an elephant in the jungle and so I read the script about Abdul without looking at the monitor to see what the film was. Pandemonium broke out in the gallery and I couldn't figure out why until I looked at the monitor to see a Japanese supermarket at Christmas.'

John Craven as he is normally seen in the studio.

The side of *Newsround* that viewers do not normally see. John Craven in the programme's office with Ali and Paul.

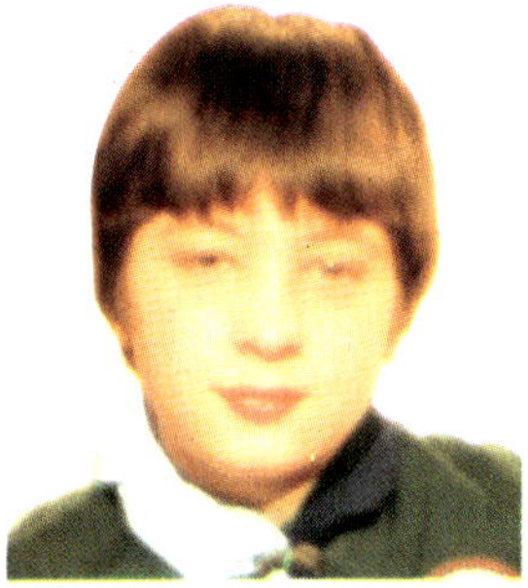

Ali: *'Do you always do an April Fools' joke on April Fools' Day?'*

John Craven: 'We do sometimes! Do you remember the one about the Panda egg when we said that London Zoo were expecting a happy event any time and that the egg had been seen? We took a lot of people in on that occasion!'

Paul: *'What do you do for relaxation?'*

John Craven: 'Well, I don't get an awful lot of free time. I like to spend time with my family when I have time off. I've two daughters and we live in the country and we like going for walks and exploring the area.

'I go around quite a lot to open things like fêtes. Last Sunday, for example, I went to the Great Western Railway Society at Didcot in Oxfordshire where there are wonderful old steam engines and carriages. They have a lot of knick-knacks and bric-a-brac and they haven't had anywhere to store them in the past. But now they have just built this museum which is beautiful, full of all these momentos, which they asked me to open. My family and I had great fun there.

'We spend a lot of time at weekends going to very interesting places. I read a lot, I watch television . . .'

Ali: *'What's your favourite programme?'*

John Craven: 'Oh, I don't think I have a particular favourite. I watch all the current affairs programmes because that's part of my job. I like comedy shows; I love *Hi-di-Hi*, *The World About Us* and old adventure films.'

Ali: *'You must obviously enjoy your job.'*

John Craven: Oh, yes, it's a lot of fun! It's funny what people say. You just do a job on the television and it's amazing what people say about you.

'I was driving into work this morning and listening to Terry Wogan on the radio. Someone had written to ask him if he thought that Imran Khan, the captain of the Pakistan Cricket Team, looked like John Craven with a suntan! I never thought that at all!

'I also enjoy working for *NEWSROUND*. It was the first regular news programme for young people in the world, and since then many countries have followed suit. I was in Japan recently and I was surprised to see the Japanese version on television!

'As I said before, I am very lucky with my job.'

Thanks for the interview

Photographs by Ted C

Alan Gordon, Editor of SCOUTING, warns you to keep your stove away from your tent — or you could be . . .

Two minutes from DEATH!

Photographs by courtesy of Geoff Wilkinson of the *Sunday Mirror*

Weekend hikes, particularly in the winter, can mean cold evenings. When it's like that, there's nothing better than snuggling into a warm sleeping bag after a late hot drink and listening to the wind whistling by outside.

If you've used a stove for cooking keep it well away from your tent – and *never* use it to warm the tent to keep the cold night at bay. Stoves in – or near – tents are death traps . . . and we'll show you just what we mean over the page.

These pictures were specially taken to demonstrate the speed with which a tent is soon reduced to a pile of ash – two minutes or less!

What sort of chance would you have if you were using a stove for cooking or for warmth inside a hike tent – and you accidently knocked it over? Your tent would soon be ablaze – and the message is a simple one. Don't take a stove inside your tent and, whatever the weather, cook outside. Don't light a stove in the entrance, but keep it well away from the tent.

A nylon tent was used for the demonstration. Flame retardant tents are available on the market, but they are more expensive, and even then they only stop a fire from spreading as quickly. And if you burn your tent, it's doubtful if it will be much use to you again.

A stove in your tent may keep you warm, but it could cost a life – *your* life!

Colin McKay says . . .

NOW THERE'S A THING, BUT PERHAPS YOU DIDN'T KNOW!

Primary

In painting the primary colours are red, blue and yellow, and they are called primary colours because all other shades can be made by mixing two or more together.

Thus red and yellow make orange, and blue and yellow make green. Black and white are not counted as colours.

In light, and therefore in television, the primary colours are red, blue and green. Red and green light together make yellow.

Poisonous

Many plants contain poisonous substances, some of which are powerful enough to kill an animal or a person eating them. In others, the poison is merely an irritant, as in the familiar stinging nettle.

Poisonous plants may be divided into plants which are always poisonous, those which are sometimes poisonous, those which are poisonous to some animals and not to others, and those which have poisonous parts.

Monkshood, deadly nightshade, yew and hemlock are always poisonous.

An example of a plant which is sometimes poisonous is the may-apple, which is poisonous when unripe, but safe when ripe. Acorns can poison cows or horses, but will make good food for pigs, while rabbits can safely eat the death cap fungus, which can kill a person.

Plants which are partly poisonous include the tomato, whose fruits are edible but whose stalks, roots and leaves are not, the potato, which has edible tubers and poisonous fruits; and rhubarb which has edible stalks, but whose leaves are deadly if cooked with salt.

This tent was specially pitched for the demonstration. The firelighter moves in swiftly to start the blaze . . .

In a matter of seconds the flames lick upwards . . .

Twenty seconds after the firelighter struck, the door is a mass of red-hot flame and already the roof is alight . . .

Stars

Stars are an incredibly long way away from us. They are so far away that we cannot talk of their distance in terms of kilometres or miles, so astronomers use much bigger units of measurement.

One of these measurements is the light-year, the distance light travels in one year. Since light moves at 299,793 kilometres (186,276 miles) a second, a light-year is about 9,700,000,000,000 kilometres!

The nearest star, which is called Proxima Centauri, is 4.3 light-years away. In other words, the light we see from it left the star about 4 years and 3 months ago.

Other units used by astronomers are the astronomical unit, which is the distance from the Earth to the Sun, about 150,000,000 kilometres (93,000,000 miles); and the parsec, which is 3.26 light-years.

Disguise

Animals that are likely to be pounced on and eaten by other animals have developed means of keeping themselves safe. Many of these involve some form of disguise.

Very few animals disguise themselves deliberately; as a rule, they are born either with the right colouring to keep them safe, or with an instinct which leads them to take protective action automatically. The simplest form of disguise is what we call 'protective colouration': the animal is coloured to look like its background. For instance, a polar bear and an Arctic fox both have white coats that do not show up on snow. The blotchy coat of a giraffe and the spots on a leopard make them hard to see in the undergrowth where there are patches of shadow and brilliant sunshine.

'Protective resemblance' is the term used when the shape of an animal matches its background. The familiar stick insect looks just like a twig, and other insects resemble leaves or stones.

'Mimicry' is the term used when one animal looks like another. It is most common in insects and is also found in the snake world. For example, some insects which are dangerous or unpleasant to eat, such as wasps, have markings of black and yellow. Many of the harmless – and edible – hoverflies are also coloured black and yellow, and for this reason birds leave them alone.

Trees

Trees can act as living calendars. If you look at the cut end of a log, you can see a series of rings. A year's growth is represented by a pair of rings, one dark (summer growth) and one light (spring

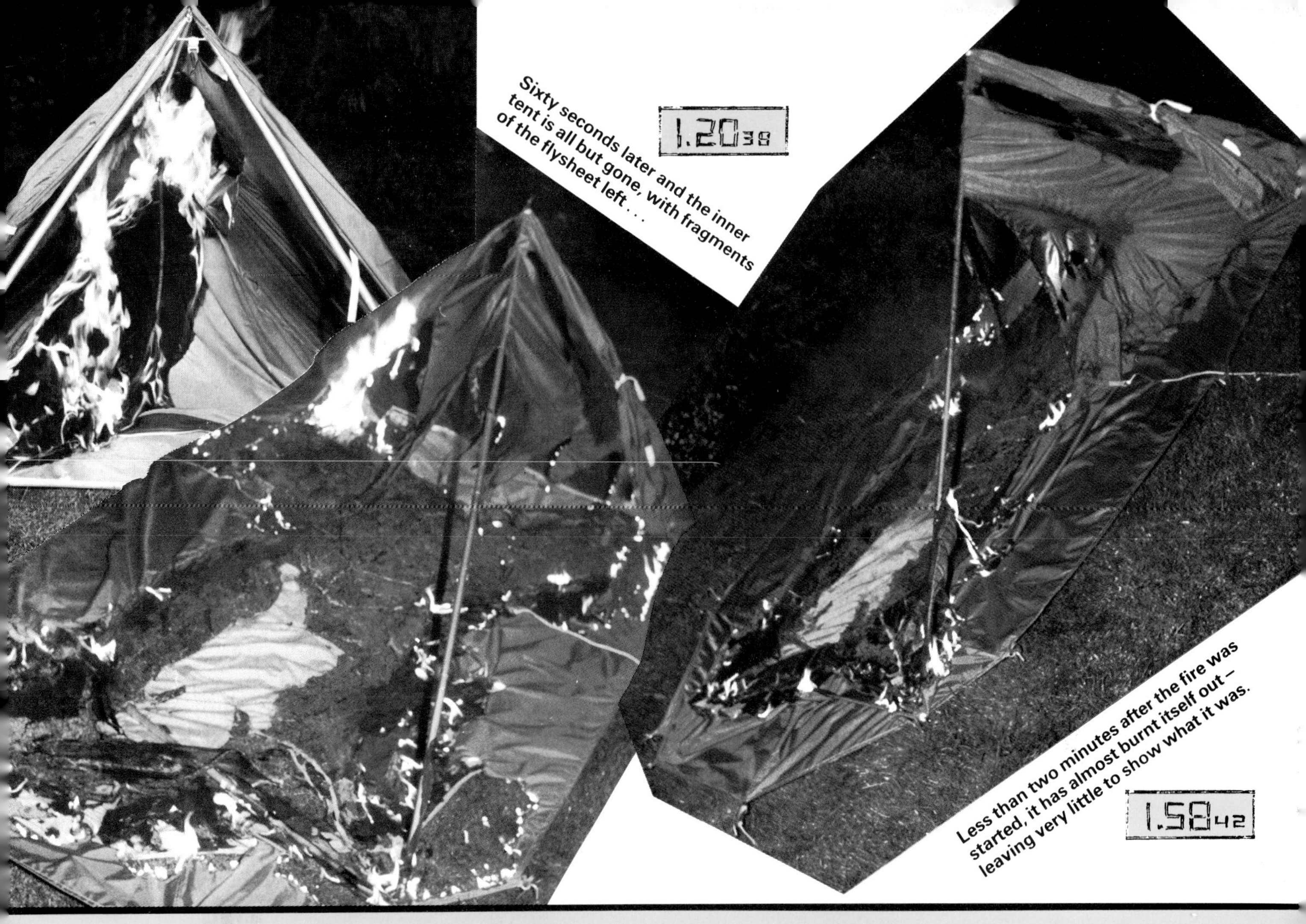

1.20 38

Sixty seconds later and the inner tent is all but gone, with fragments of the flysheet left . . .

Less than two minutes after the fire was started, it has almost burnt itself out – leaving very little to show what it was.

1.58 42

growth). Narrow rings show dry years, and wider ones years with plenty of rain.

By counting the rings you can tell a tree's age – and the weather for each year of its life also shows in the width of the rings.

With the aid of long-lived species such as the bristlecone pines – some of which are more than 4,000 years old – scientists now have tree calendars going back a very long way. By matching wood from old buildings with the known tree calendars, they can say when the building was put up.

The study of tree-rings is called dendrochronology, from two Greek words meaning 'tree' and 'time'.

Two young Scouts, busily using this tree stump to rest their notebooks on, could find out how old the tree was before it was felled. This feature tells you how.

Photograph by Ron Jeffries

Do you know who Shirley Crabtree is? Would you enjoy eating escargots? And what's a colporteur?

To find out try . . .

JAD'S Quiz

'A Scout has courage in all difficulties' — and you might just need some courage when you tackle this Quiz. The questions aren't easy — a few of them you may be able to answer straight away, but for others you may need help from other Scouts in your Patrol or your parents, and for some you may even need to spend an hour or two in the reference library. But to get the most fun out of the Quiz, have a real go and try to work out the answers for yourself before you look at page 62 for the answers.

1. Who said "Bother!" and then "Oh, deary me!"?
2. 25th March, 24th June, 29th September, . . .what is the missing date?
3. Which British counties are these?

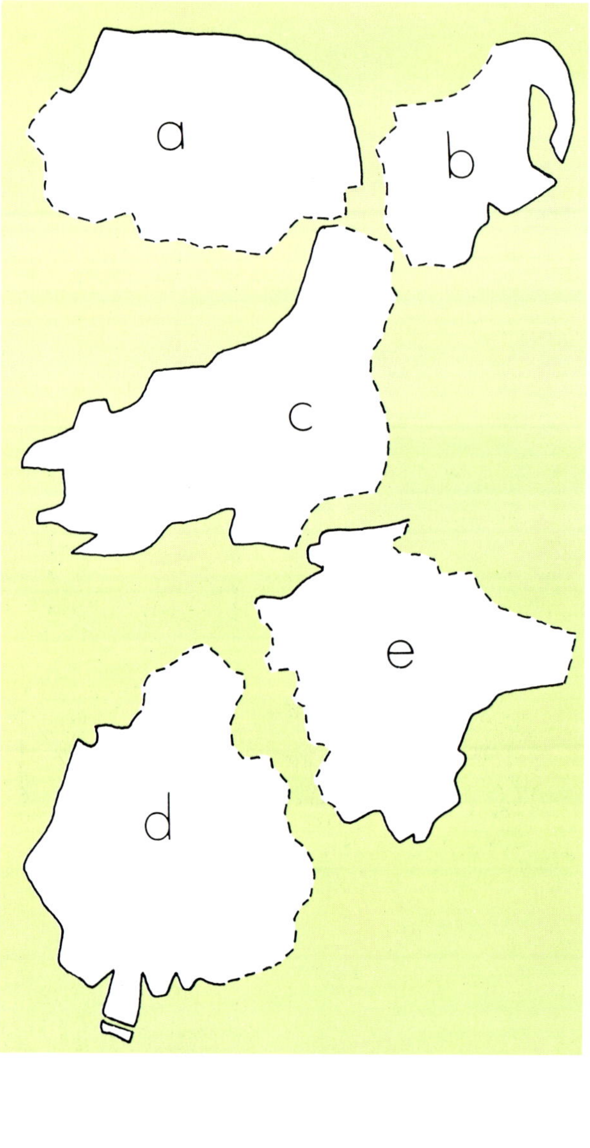

4. Two Eskimos are sitting outside their igloo. The big Eskimo is the little Eskimo's father, but the little Eskimo is *not* the big Eskimo's son. How is this possible?
5. For what do we particularly remember (a) the *Beagle*, (b) the *Discovery*, (c) the *Forfarshire*, (d) the *Golden Hind*, (e) the *Hermes*, and (f) the *Santa Maria*?
6. If C = 6, H = 1 and 0 = 8, what does U equal?
7. Identify these Camp Fire songs:

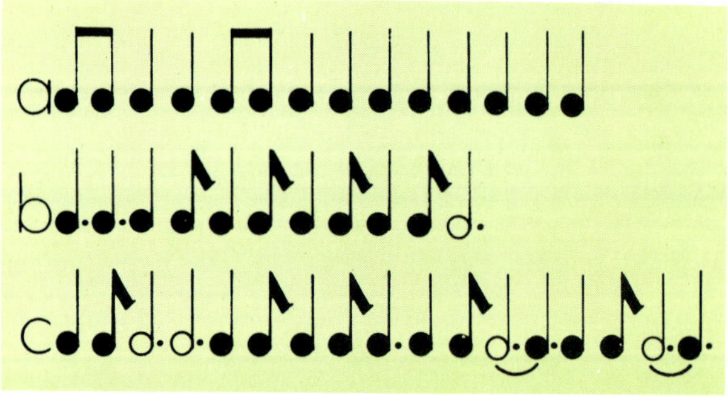

8. Where would you go to see the Gunners, the Rams, the Pilgrims, the Dons or the Canaries at home?
9. If you were given an Apple, a Pet or a Spectrum, what would you do with it?
10. If it takes five minutes to boil one egg, how long does it take to boil three eggs?
11. Where might you greet someone with the words (a) Guten Morgen, (b) Bore da, (c) Bonjour, (d) Buenos dias, or (e) **Заравствуйте**?
12. Who *wasn't* Major William Martin, R.M.?
13. How are Shirley Crabtree, Marion Morrison, Harry Webb, Karol Wojtyla and Eric Bartholomew and Ernest Wiseman better known?

14. (a) In which sport does eight-ninths of each team go backwards?
    (b) In which sport does the winning team (only) go backwards?
15. Which is the better swimmer — a bloater or a kipper?
16. What sort of weather does each of these symbols represent?

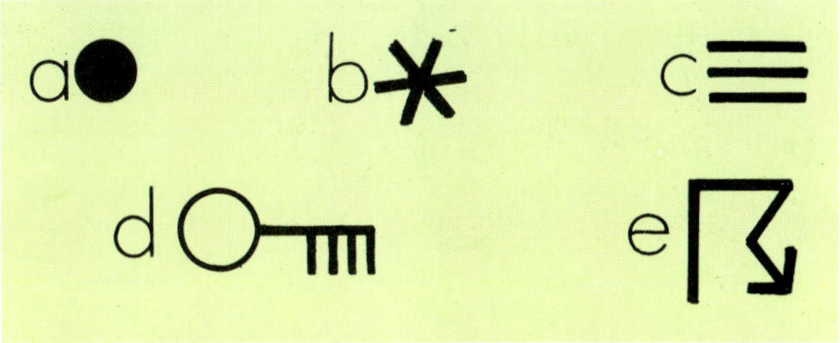

17. Now I want a drink (orangeade is lovely) after the great problems involving relative mechanics— but what has that got to do with circles?
18. If Henry and Edward are equal top with eight each, George has six and John and Anne each have only one, how many each have James, Charles and Elizabeth?
19. A plank four metres long is cut exactly in half; how long is each half? (And the answer is *not* two metres!)
20. Identify these knots, and say what each one is used for:

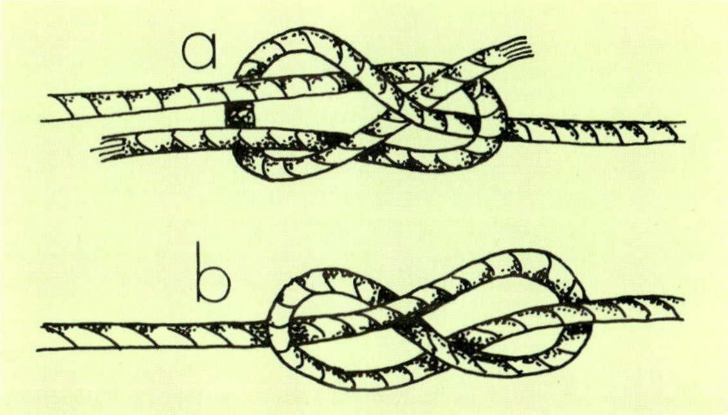

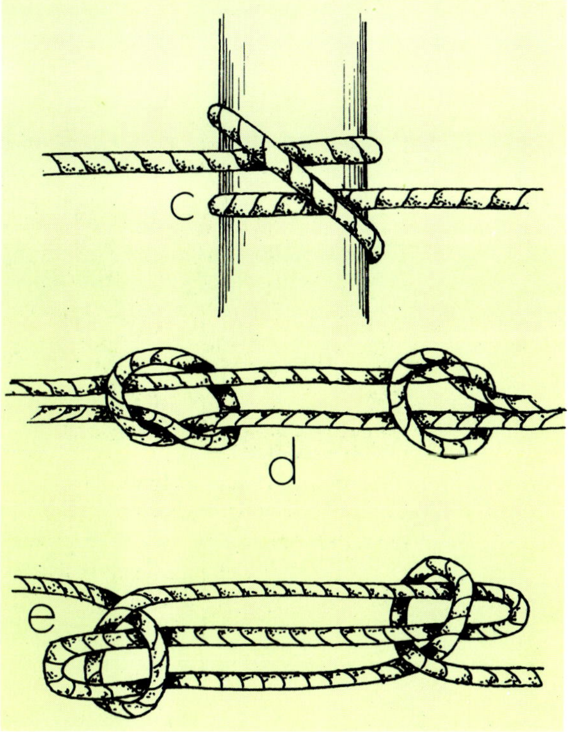

21. Who have green heads, blue hands and very unseaworthy boats?
22. If you ordered *escargots, bouillabaisse, grenouilles* and *pommes frites* from a French menu, what would you get?
23. If John always tells the truth and James always lies, and one of them says (about the other) "He says he's called James," which one is speaking?
24. A bottle and a cork together cost 11p. The bottle costs 10p more than the cork — how much does the cork cost?
25. What sort of work does a lapidary do? And what about a cordwainer? A farrier? A chandler? A colporteur?
26. Why should Winston Smith be especially interested in this year's *Scout Annual*?

27. Here in code are the names of six trees — try to decode them:

28. Who, where or what is an ampersand?

29. Why were there no births, marriages or deaths anywhere in Great Britain between 3rd September and 13th September, 1752?

30. If you are given 4 oz. flour, an egg, ½ pint milk, a knob of butter and a frying pan, what is the best thing to make with them?

31. What games are normally played on areas marked out like these?

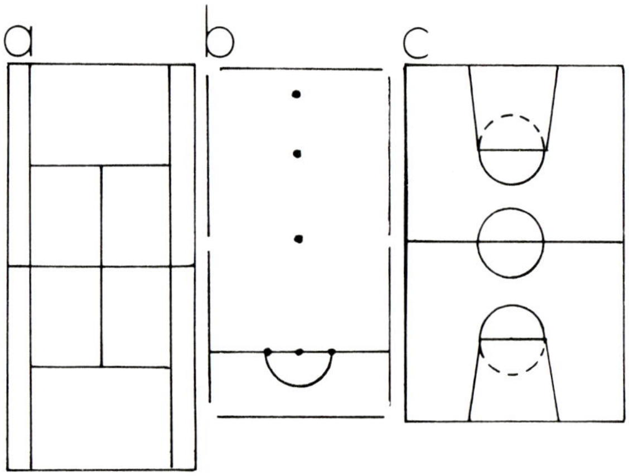

32. What do the initials A.A., B.B., C.C., D.D., and E.E. stand for?

33. Does a kilogram of pure water weigh more or less when it is frozen?

34. In a village street the butcher, the baker, the grocer and the chemist have adjoining shops; their names (not in the same order) are Matthew, Mark, Luke and John. Luke and John shave themselves each morning, but the chemist is shaved by the village barber. Matthew and John often play darts against the chemist and the baker. John's shop is between the baker's and the grocer's. Which shop is kept by the man with the beard?

35. If the 119th is the longest, which one is the shortest?

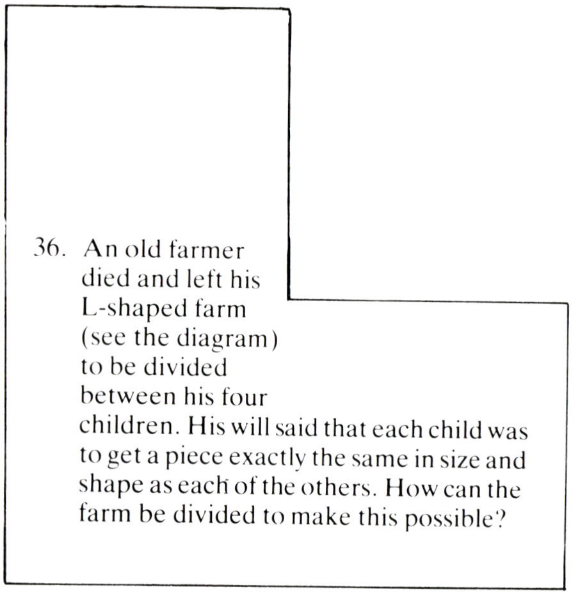

36. An old farmer died and left his L-shaped farm (see the diagram) to be divided between his four children. His will said that each child was to get a piece exactly the same in size and shape as each of the others. How can the farm be divided to make this possible?

37. What sort of information could you find in *Brewer*? in *Debrett*? in *Jane*?

38. William Hartnell, Patrick Troughton, Jon Pertwee, Tom Baker . . . who comes next?

39. Adrian has the same number of sisters as he has brothers, but his sister Alison has twice as many brothers as she has sisters. How many children are there in the family altogether?

40. Which Boy won the V.C. at the Battle of Jutland, and what is the connection with present-day Scouting?

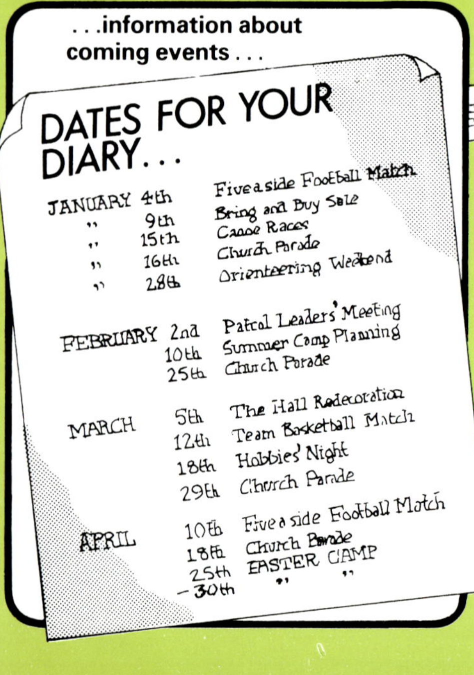

"'Whizz Kid ~ What's your 20?' asks Treetops"

by Denys J. Branch

'Treetops' was a passenger in a car towing a caravan and on his way to a national caravan rally at Sandringham, Norfolk — the home of Her Majesty the Queen.

As he got nearer the rally his CB set — which for most of the journey through East Anglia had been quiet — started to crackle into life.

Messages spun through the air with 'Milk Tray' calling 'Goldilocks', 'Teapot' wanting to chat with 'Lightning Kid', and 'Dragon Slayer' responding to 'Whizz Kid'.

'Whizz Kid' was answered when he asked for a "copy on the 10 4" — and so 'Treetops' met 'Whizz Kid' while they were still two miles apart.

CB (Citizens' Band Radio) was illegal at one time, but now a licence is available from the post office and it's becoming a popular way of communicating with friends — and of making new ones, too.

The more expensive sets are often operated from people's homes or cars, and can receive messages and transmit over several miles. There are cheaper sets which can be held in the hand and work well over shorter distances. The very cheapest are often sold in pairs and have a range of perhaps two hundred yards, but they're good for use in camp in wide games or between Patrol tents.

CB reception in towns can be bad, particularly in the early evening immediately after school. Homework is often discussed between school friends. Other CB set owners just want to chat with anyone — and "anyone for a copy" or similar calls tend to block the main transmitting channel — channel 14.

'Whizz Kid' (Mark Haddleton of the 2nd Northolt Scouts) and 'Dragon Slayer' (Paul Whitney of the 5th Harlington Scouts) have 'an eyeball' after meeting on air two miles before arriving at the national caravan rally in Norfolk.

Language

The first time you listen to messages on CB it all sounds like a foreign language with callers asking for "a 9" or saying "it's a 4" or wanting "a 10 36". With the help of a CB enthusiast or a book things become a little clearer!

CB language started in the United States of America with long distance lorry drivers talking to one another. To save time — and to make things easier — common expressions were given numbers and the 'Ten Code' was born.

If someone asked for "a 9" it meant that they wanted the previous message repeated, "a 4" was "O.K. message received" and a request for a "10 36" was a quick way of asking the time!

The 'Ten Code' is extensive, but most CB operators only use a small number of its calls. For those wanting something more detailed, there's a '13 Code', but few people remember or use it.

Lifesaving

With forty different channels to use on the majority of CB sets, channel 14 (or 'window 14' as it's sometimes called) is used to make contact with friends. Once that first contact has been made, a switch to another channel that's not already in use by others is arranged — and then talk becomes quite simple.

Some channels are restricted by arrangement. Long distance lorry drivers tend to use channel 19 for their messages and everyone respects this.

Channel 9 is the emergency channel. In most towns CB clubs arrange for someone to listen in on this channel throughout the day and

CB is a good way to meet new friends — and 'White Snake' demonstrates his rig to 'Whizz Kid'.

night for emergency messages. Many drivers who have seen an accident or an incident such as a bank raid have called channel 9 and passed on a message which has saved lives or helped the police to get to the scene more quickly.

Scout Troops could well consider setting up their own listening stations for — as we discovered at the national caravan rally — many Scouts are CB enthusiasts. 'Whizz Kid' was Mark Haddleton of the 2nd Northolt and 'Dragon Slayer' turned out to be Paul Whitney of the 5th Harlington. They arranged to meet — or have 'an eyeball' in CB language.

During this rally — where more than 12,000 people were living in caravans — a fire broke out close to a marquee. A CB enthusiast spotted it and called for help on channel 9 — with the result that the fire brigade got there in double quick time!

CB's range is limited and it's doubtful if it will ever become a major means of communication like the telephone or telex. With so many people using it in large towns it can become jumbled, but it's great fun to use and a way of making friends. It does have a use, too, for lifesaving.

It should be used carefully and nothing should be done to upset other people. Never send false messages, for you could be misunderstood and something that you intended as a joke could go badly wrong.

If you or other Scouts in your Troop are interested, make contact in the first place with your local CB club. And don't forget that licence from the post office before you start chatting away on 'window 14'!

'Whizz Kid' chats on his CB set, while 'Dragon Slayer' tries to find out what's going on.

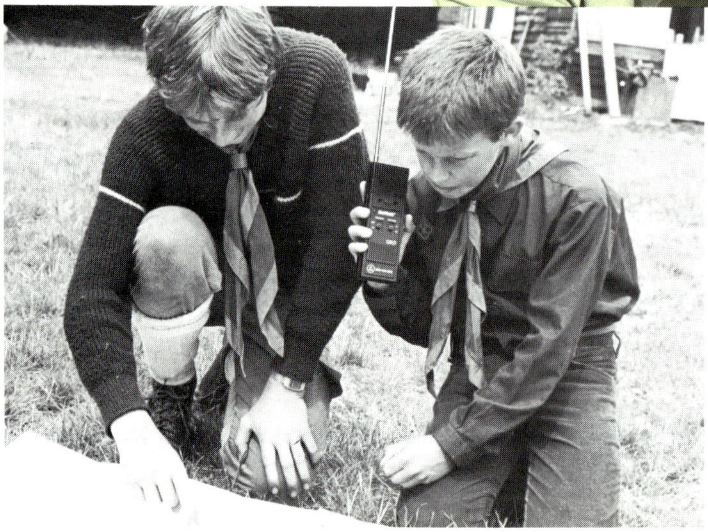

Stephen Pettitt and Peter Spencer of the 5th Prittlewell Scout Troop study their map at Belchamps, their County Camp Site. Later they arranged to meet their Patrol at an agreed spot — by sending a message on their hand-held CB set. With a range of two miles or so, these are ideal for keeping in touch with the rest of the Patrol on a hike or in Troop wide games.

Alternatively, you could sell advertising space . . .

Keep your charges low and you should be able to get some advertisements. Parents may be able to help with this and local shopkeepers might take space.

Step 5: How will you distribute your newsletter?

Will you hand it out at Troop Meetings, post copies or deliver by hand?

A newsletter is a useful way to keep everyone in the Troop informed.

Keep the content light and interesting — and attractively presented.

Have a team of people working on it — editor, reporters, typist, production manager, distributor, etc.
Make sure you can afford to keep your newsletter going. See that your readers receive their copies regularly and in good time for the events you are telling them about.

Send copies to your local newspaper, your Sponsoring Authority, members of the Group Council, your District Commissioner, County Commissioner and Scout Headquarters . . . in fact, to anyone who might be interested!
Happy writing!

JUST A FIELD...

Written and illustrated by Bill Bruce

When you arrive at a new camp site all that faces you is a field – just an area of grass, a few trees and the surrounding hedges. Before long, you've pitched your tents, marked out the Patrol sites and kitchen areas and created a 'village under canvas' – no longer just a field.

But it was never 'just a field'... there's more going on in that area of grass with its surrounding hedges and trees than you would ever imagine.

Perhaps one of the best times to see some of the activity is first thing in the morning. As dawn breaks, poke your head out of the tent flap and just look and listen...

The Dawn Chorus

The first thing that you will probably hear is the chorus as all the birds living in the trees and hedgerows burst into song to welcome the new day. You may find it hard to spot the individual birds, hidden in the foliage, but in time you may learn to recognise their calls.

Under the surface of the whole field are the worms... up to three million of them in a single acre. They normally live about three or four inches below the surface, but in the early morning they may still be out on the grass having been up for most of the night, looking for leaves and decaying matter. The early birds may break off their singing to fly down and catch a worm for breakfast. Sometimes you may find worms floundering around in puddles, and this once led to the 'old wives' tale' that worms fell in the rain!

Flowers Amongst the Grass

Many fields have a high proportion of rye grass growing in them. It is favoured by farmers as it gives good hay for livestock feeding in the winter. Rye grass tends to grow tall and is very sturdy, quickly springing back into shape if flattened.

In amongst the grass are all sorts of flowers and in the early morning they are just beginning to open. There can be around thirty or forty different wild plants in any field, but you will probably find mainly two or three.

The best known flowers are easy to spot. Dandelions are among the most common and can be quite useful as you can eat the leaves – but check on how they should be washed and cooked before you try! Later in the day, why not 'tell the time' by blowing at one of the fluffy seed-heads?

Clover is very widespread in the fields and comes in two main varieties, red and white. It grows low to the ground and is often obscured by taller grasses. Both varieties have groups of three oval leaves, and St. Patrick, the Patron Saint of Ireland, used clover to illustrate the Holy Trinity – three in one. You can spend many hours searching for four-leafed varieties. They *do* sometimes occur and are supposed to bring you great luck but they are more likely to bring rheumatism from kneeling in the wet grass!

Some things that grow around the field may look like mushrooms – but do not be tempted to eat any of them. There are over 10,000 species of fungi growing in this country and the majority of them are poisonous, so the best thing to do is leave them all alone – just in case!

All sorts of insects live in the field and many may have crept into your tent – coaxed out of their normal habitat by the warmth. Look for all the insects shown in the illustration and try to identify as many as you can.

Of the large creatures living amongst the grass, you are most likely to see slugs and snails. Slugs are basically snails without shells and as they will eat almost anything, you may often see them moving slowly across the grass devouring everything in their path.

Although you will often see a snail you may also hear a strange sound early in the morning – a regular *'tap-tap-tap'*, followed by a thud. It's a thrush cracking open a snail's shell in an effort to eat the soft creature inside.

The Food Chain

A field forms a complete 'food-chain' and you should be able to study at least part of it. The smallest insects are eaten by the larger ones and they are eaten by the birds. The plants are eaten by the insects and slugs and they in turn are eaten by the birds and small animals. Then the larger animals take their turn and you may even catch a glimpse of a fox as it creeps back to its den early in the morning. High overhead the kestrels hover motionless, hoping to make a meal of a scurrying mouse or vole.

The field itself may be there to act as food. Try to find out if the grass is for grazing or for hay or silage for winter feeds. What grew in the field last year? Was it always grazing or has it ever grown wheat or barley?

The illustration overleaf shows many of the things that may be in your field. Try to identify as many as you can before you look at the key below.

The next time you go camping – remember – there's a great deal really going on in all that grass so don't think that it's 'just a field'.

Key

1. Pheasant; 2. Magpie; 3. Fieldfare; 4. Jay; 5. Long-eared Owl; 6. Crow; 7. Kestrel; 8. Song Thrush; 9. Rooks; 10. Lapwing; 11. Wood Pigeon; 12. Blackbird; 13. Pipistrelle Bat; 14. Rabbits; 15. Hare; 16. Fox; 17. Stag Beetle; 18. Green Tiger Beetle; 19. Two-spot Ladybird; 20. Violet Ground Beetle; 21. Woodlouse; 22. Devil's Coach Horse; 23. Centipede; 24. Millipede; 25. Scarlet-tipped Flower Beetle; 26. Earwig; 27. Seven-spot Ladybird; 28. Poppy; 29. Creeping Buttercup; 30. Thistle; 31. Meadow Cranesbill, 32. Destroying Angel; 33. Fly Agaric; 34. Field Mushroom; 35. Dandelion.

Note:
It is highly unlikely that all of these would ever be found together in one field, but you should be able to see most of them at some time or another. The items illustrated are not to scale.

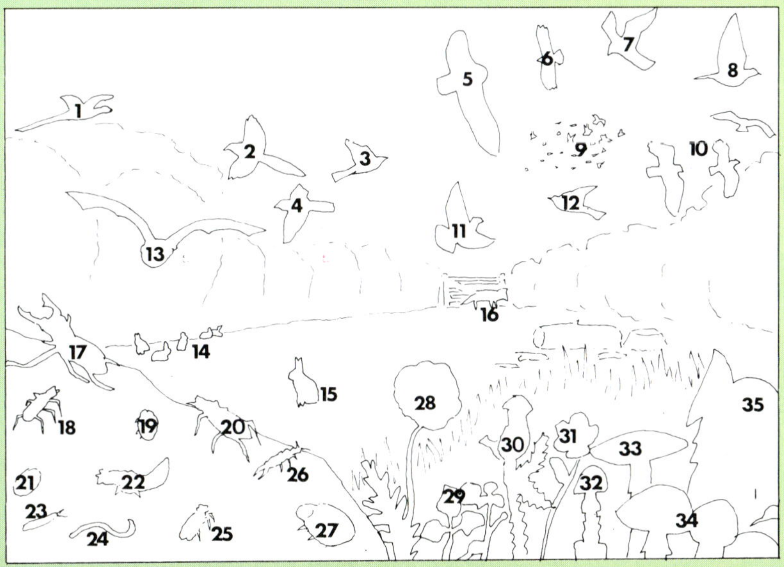

JUST A FIELD...
BILL BRUCE 82

PLANT PASTIMES

Written and illustrated by Anthony Wootton

There's a lot of fun to be had from using natural materials to create a variety of simple games and activities. Here are just a few — and others will occur to you when you start looking around the countryside in late summer and autumn.

Most of these I made as a boy living in rural Buckinghamshire. They require the simplest of things — weeds from the hedgerow, pea-pods after peas have been shelled from the garden, conkers, acorns and so on. Take care when you collect any of these in the countryside — don't hack or throw things into trees to bring down conkers or acorns; look for the wild plants we've mentioned here in hedgerows and only take what you need to experiment — remember that some plants are rare. Ask permission before going to search for materials on private land.

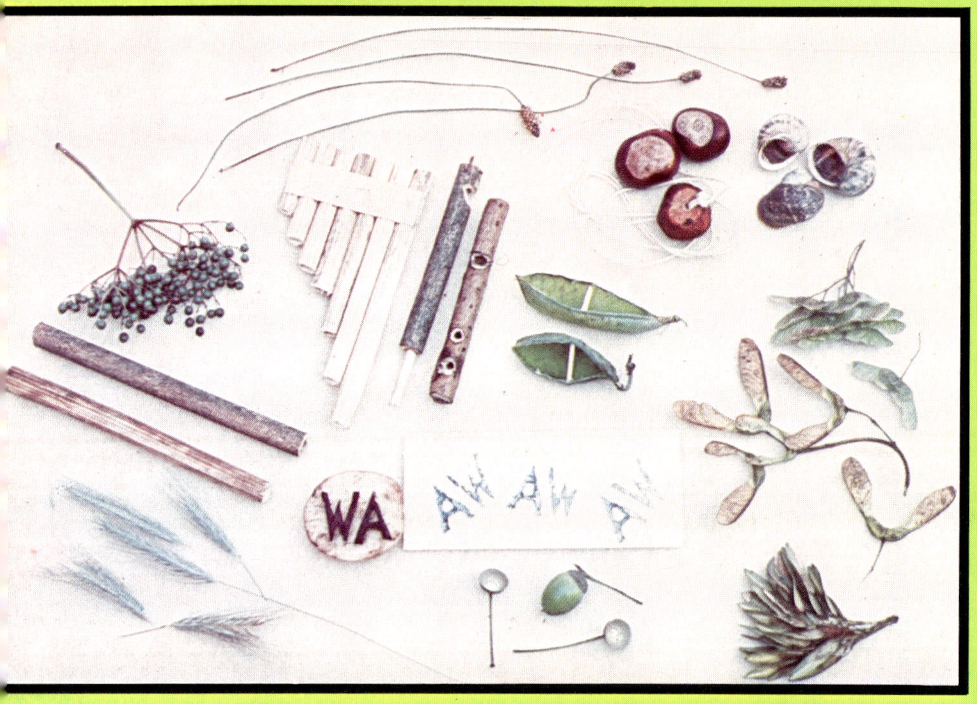

(Top) **ribwort plantain seed stalks for plantain pop-gun:** *(top left)* **unripe elder fruits make good ammunition for the pea-shooters of elder and hogwood stems:** *(below left)* **wild barley darts:** *(top right)* **horse chestnut conkers and empty snail shells:** *(centre left)* **pan-pipes of hogweed stems, elder wood whistles:** *(centre right)* **pea-pod boats:** *(right)* **aeroplanes of field maple, sycamore and ash seeds:** *(centre below)* **potato stamp:** *(bottom centre)* **acorn pipes.**

A plantain pop-gun.

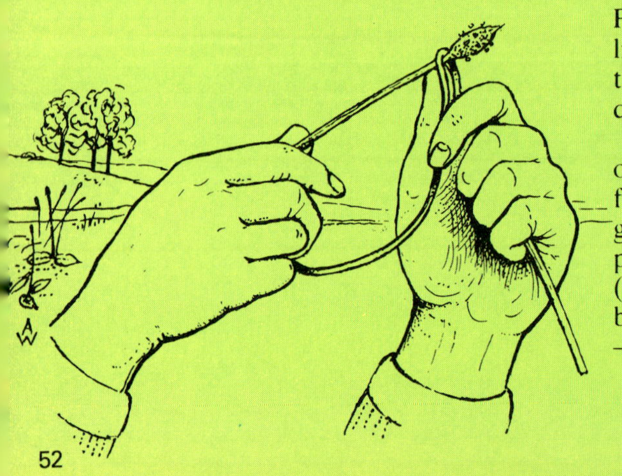

Plantain pop-gun

Popular in summer, they require little or no making (like many of the items described here), but quite a bit of skill in performance!

All you'll need is a supply of plantains — weeds which frequently cause heartache to groundsmen on sports and playing fields. Ribwort plantain (*Plantago lanceolata*) is the best because of its rounder seed-heads — other species tend to have longer seed-heads. Look it up in a book on wild plants if you are uncertain.

Loop the plantain stem about itself to form a collar just behind the seed-head and then pull sharply — pointing the head at your target. Have a competition using a bowl or bucket, and see who gets the most seed-heads into it.

Wild barley darts

These, again, involve no making. Collect a supply of ripe seed-heads of wild wall barley (*Hordeum marinum*) which grows commonly by the wayside, near old walls and the like. Break them up into lengths of about two inches (50mm) and they make excellent missiles. Avoid the face, but they stick well on clothes!

Pea-shooters

The stems of hedge parsley or hogweed are already hollow and can simply be cut to the required length. Again, look them up in a book of wild plants — and avoid giant hogweed (for the juice can cause skin irritation) and hemlock (which is poisonous and has spotted stems).

More permanent shooters can be made from elder stems: they contain pith, but this is easily pushed out. The unripe seeds of the elder are ideal to blow through the stems.
They are often available in large numbers — clusters or umbels which eventually ripen into those juicy blue-black fruits from which wine is commonly made.

Conkers

Some will soak their 'sixers' in vinegar to make them harder. Others put their conkers in a warm oven for a while for the same effect. It's a good idea to make the hole in the chestnut with a hot skewer to avoid premature cracking. Put the conker onto a pad of firm cloth and press downwards with the skewer — *never* do it in your hand.

Did you know, by the way, that the original conkers are supposed to have been empty garden snail shells? 'Conker' is, in fact, a snail shell in country dialects in some parts of England, notably in Worcestershire. Some people think the word is onomatopoeic — it reflects the sound made when two chestnuts (or snail shells!) clash together.
But perhaps it's more simple than that and the word 'conker' is merely a corruption of 'conquer'.

Pea-pod boats

My father grew his own peas, so in early summer when these became available, a few of the largest and straightest pods would be used to make simple boats.

Open the pod on the upper, slightly concave side, eat or cook the peas, and wedge bits of matchstick across as seats.
We had a lot of fun with these 'redskin canoes' in an old water butt! Add a mast and sail.

Whistles

Make these from the same materials as the pea-shooters. Cut a V-shaped notch near one end and two smaller, round holes near the other to form 'stops'.

Place a semi-circular piece of wood in the V-shaped notch — it needs to fit tightly and you can make it from a smaller twig split down the middle. You blow down the mouth — the end where you made the V-shaped notch.

A more elaborate whistle is made by cutting a piece of ash or willow twig. You tap it all along its length and soak it in water to loosen the bark (twigs are best collected in spring when the sap is rising and the bark looser).
After a while you should be able to slide the bark off the wood in one piece. The wooden core can then be moved up and down the bark sheath so as to alter the pitch of the notes produced.

Pan-pipes can be made from hollow reeds and other plant stems, binding them together in different lengths. An extremely simple sort of whistle can be made from various kinds of wide-leaved grasses. You simply take a section between your thumbs and blow hard — but it takes practice!

A whistle made from elder stem.

Potato stamps

Cut a potato in half and carve out a design with a knife. Try your initials or your Patrol's sign, but you have to remember to cut in reverse if the letters are to come out the right way round when you print them. Spread water-colours or inks onto the design and print down onto paper.

Sycamore aeroplanes and acorn pipes

It's intriguing the way plants and trees disperse their seeds. If you throw a winged sycamore seed into the air, it falls to the ground with a very distinctive whirling motion — the seeds of field maple and the one-winged seeds of the ash do the same. It all works better if there's a bit of wind and seed dispersal relies on this, since the seeds' wings may carry them a considerable distance, helping the species to spread.

Acorn pipes are really just whimsy! We used to stick the little stemmed acorn cups in the corner of our mouths and pretend we were old chaps smoking a pipe of baccy. At least this doesn't need a Government health- warning!

Fox and Geese

This is a simple board game for two players and it dates back to the 13th century in Britain.
Draw up the board as shown on this page and make thirteen counters for the geese, with a larger one for the fox.

The geese are always placed to one side of the board and the fox takes up the centre spot. The idea is either for the fox to take the geese by jumping over them onto a vacant point beyond, or for the geese to move up in formation and eventually hem the fox in so that it can't move at all.
Moves can be made along any straight line, both forwards and back. The game can be varied by making much larger boards with many more geese and two foxes.
But I'd try the simple version first, which I think is the best anyway.

The board and counters for 'Fox and Geese'.

Hiking is a great way to see the countryside. Dave Siddons — and a Patrol of Leicestershire Scouts — show you how to . . .

GO HIKING- WITH YOUR PATROL!

Next to camping, the most basic of Scout activities must be hiking, and it's one that you can easily organise in your Patrol. It's a great way for your Patrol to get out into the country — and will give you a lot of fun.

The Patrol-in-Council is the place to plan the hike. There are several things to arrange and, if the hike is to be a success, it's essential that the planning is done properly.

The points to decide are . . .

- When shall we go? (for it's no use organising a hike if no one can go!)
- Where shall we go?
- What shall we do?
- What shall we take?
- How will we get there?
- What shall we eat?

When all these things are decided, the Patrol Leader should have all the details written down (one copy for each Scout), so that everyone (and not least your parents) know what's going on.

I hope you will take up the suggestions in this article — and that you have lots of fun on your Patrol hike.

What shall we do?

You may just want to hike for hiking's sake, but most Scouts like to do something else on the hike. The sort of activities you could include are . . .

* A visit to a castle, watermill, farm museum, site of a battle, church;
* Swimming;
* Boating;
* Barbecue;
* Sketching;
* Collecting leaves, bird-spotting;

The Patrol hike is a great opportunity to put your map reading and compass skills to good use.

Where shall we go?

Much depends on what you want to do!
You won't do much boating if you go somewhere without boats — and water is important if you want to go swimming!
So plan your route carefully, using an Ordnance Survey map. Check that you can achieve the aims of your hike on the route. For example, if you want to visit a castle, find out about opening times before you go.
Remember, a hike is not intended to be a route march! About 15 kilometres is ample for a normal day's hike.
Avoid walking along roads and follow public footpaths wherever possible. One Scout needs to be in charge of the route — and he uses the map and compass to guide the Patrol accurately.
If you intend to do a more adventurous type of hike and go into mountainous country, then you will have to take special precautions and your Scout Leader will be able to put you in contact with people who can offer advice.

If you can find a good spot — in this case a pebble beach on the edge of a river — it's great to have a mini-barbecue for lunch.

On their hike the Patrol took advantage of the cool water of the River Derwent in Cumbria to have a paddle!

When shall we go?

Obviously, weekend or holiday-time!
One other possibility is to mount a Patrol hike from your Troop's Summer Camp, but this needs to be agreed at the Patrol Leaders' Council.

How shall we get there?

Hikes rarely start or finish from home — so you'll need some transport.
* Cycle: This is the ideal method, although you will need to make some arrangements beforehand about leaving your cycles at a farm or similar place while you are hiking. One problem is that your route will have to be circular, so that you come back to your starting point to collect your cycles to ride home. The advantage is that you are not dependent on anyone else for transport.
* Bus or train: This is the next best — but it can be expensive. You'll need to make very careful enquiries about times and fares.
Be careful not to rely on the last bus back — only to find that you've missed it!
* Dad's car: This is often the most convenient method, but it relies heavily on whether or not Dad is available. You need to try to become independent of other people, so this is only a third best means of transport.
* Skip's car: This is the worst method — although the one most frequently used. It's the worst method because your Scout Leader is trying to get you to do things for yourself, and he feels a certain sense of failure if he is called on to carry you about. Nevertheless, it does have the advantage that he is used to having his car full of muddy Scouts and kit!

Light your fire down by the water's edge — but clear away every trace before you move off on your hike again.

What shall we eat?

Food is important to all Scouts! You can, of course, take the easy way out, and have sandwiches and a bottle of pop. It's also a good idea to take high energy foods — like chocolate and boiled sweets — to eat as you go along. It's far better, though, to take a small stove or two, and cook yourselves something on the way. Provided that you get permission first, you could light a fire and cook your lunch on that.

Many old churches have interesting things to look at. This gravestone is in a one-thousand-year-old churchyard.

Signposts can often be helpful — but never rely on them. Always check carefully with the map.

What shall we wear?

Much depends on the weather and the time of year.
Boots and two pairs of thick socks are essential, and so too, is a waterproof cagoule with a hood.
In summer, shorts are better than long trousers, but you need to take spare sweaters at any time of year.
In winter, you will need gloves and extra warm clothing. Scout uniform is definitely not suitable for hikes, but you will want to identify yourselves as Scouts and to look efficient. Each Scout should wear a Scout Badge prominently.
Extra clothing, food, etc., should be carried in a small rucsac.

Sample of a letter to Scouts and their parents . . .

Owl Patrol Adventure hike - Sunday, June 3rd 1984

Meet at the Den at 0900hrs.

Bring spare sweater, cagoule.

Wear activity kit (T-shirt, shorts, boots and thick socks).

We shall be back at the Den by 1800hrs.

Route. We shall catch a Bus to Husband's Bosworth, then hike to the Battlefield at Naseby where the Vicar has agreed to show us the relics of the battle.
We shall return by bus from Market Harborough.

Food Pete is bringing all the food, but bring your own drink.
Kevin is organising the cooking equipment and stoves.

Queries Ring Jim (86241).

What shall we take?

Apart from the items required for your Patrol's own special activity, the Patrol will need:

* First aid kit (plasters, cotton wool, antiseptic lotion, crepe bandage, scissors, gauze and bandages);
* Silva-type compass;
* Map (preferably the 1:25000 scale);
* Small torch (just in case you are late!);
* Money for emergency 'phone call to home or Skip!

When the Patrol is on the hike, it's a good thing to share carrying the rucsac holding the main gear — then everyone gets a turn and no one becomes over-tired.

CAMP FIRE FOR THE PATROL!

Tony Allen   Illustrated by Cecil

There's nothing like sitting round a good fire in camp! But to enjoy the experience you will want to make sure the fire is ablaze and not a flop.
Like everything else in Scouting there is an art to preparing a fire for fun or for food. It's rather dangerous, to say the least, if it isn't constructed carefully.

Turn back to pages 36 and 37 where Dave Siddons has shown you how to prepare a camp fire. Avoid using the fire until the evening: a fire constructed for cooking or burning rubbish isn't going to provide the attraction of one that's been specially made ready.

What shall we do?

What about a programme for the camp fire? If you only have a few Scouts around the fire the 'entertainment' should not be too formal!
You may not wish to sing the traditional songs either — but there's lots you can do.
B.-P. suggested that the camp fire should be a quiet time to talk about the day in camp and to plan for tomorrow. What a great idea!

In between there could be a game or a yarn, or why not encourage a few questions . . . about anything? Something to eat is important, too, but perhaps that needs to be carefully considered if you intend to make the camp fire part of evening meal or supper. Cooking on the same fire really isn't on!

Let's think about a few games with a song or two thrown in. Why not make up a few words about a rival Patrol to a well-known tune? Better still, if you have a musical instrument join in what the player can play. So often a Scout with his guitar is expected to play all the camp fire songs without notice and without music. If you have a musical instrument — leave it to the player. He will know a few tunes, we hope!

One great idea is to think of some new words for camp. Devise a new name for a 'chopper of wood' or a 'carrier of water' or a person who likes toasting bread or drinking cold tea. What about a new name for an old game played in camp? Use these terms in the song *Quartermaster's Stores*.
Perhaps you can become more scientific in your approach. A space age theme might be appropriate, though much will depend on the type of camp you have experienced. You may want to sing about the weather!

What shall we eat?

What happens if the rain comes down?
Please don't retreat into the depths of a tent; unless the rain is very heavy you can still enjoy a short time round the fire. Put a few potatoes in the embers (scrub skins first) or perhaps an apple in cooking foil (seal all round the fruit) or chestnuts . . . or drop scones, or pancakes or twists of dough on a green stick. (Use the embers!)

Perhaps you have a better idea?

I suggest you arrange for a hot drink . . . on a cooking stove nearby might be safer than using a big pot on the edge of the embers.

There are lots of ways you can entertain yourselves when the songs and jokes and food are over. Why not invent a crazy-type kit list; or join in a game of *My Grandmother Went to Paris* (you add an item each as the game 'travels' round the fireside). Or you might dress up as Ancient Britons for your camp fire! What about devising an action song to sing at a Troop occasion; or your own alphabet for use by a caveman?

What about inviting another Patrol to join you later when the potatoes are ready for eating; or doing the cooking on another fire nearby? One of the best camp fires I remember was one where we had two fires — one for warmth (to our backs!) and one for singing around.

You will have attended a large scale camp fire where Scouts (and Leaders) wear camp fire blankets and all the trimmings. There is an art in putting together a programme so that there is a choice of song! An action song (there's an idea for your mini-camp fire) and a round (perhaps difficult for five or six Scouts!), a cumulative song (it just goes on repeating) or a spiritual (perhaps you might hum the tune of one of those at your fire).

Here are a few ideas for songs . . . if you dare! Add your own verses to *What Shall We Do With a Drunken Sailor?*, *Michael Row the Boat Ashore*, *Kum-by-ya*, etc, or *A Poor Old Man was Crossing the Road* (then you add 'vehicles' to knock him down).

Oh, and finish with a prayer. "Thank you, God, for a great time in camp; for the fellowship round the flames of our camp fire." That's the real purpose of the camp fire . . . to reflect about the world and you and your camp!

David James tells Geoff Platt . . .

I'm in the Church Youth Club because. . .

Not all the organisations you can join wear uniforms and have badges. Youth clubs don't, for example, and there are many of these around the country, some run by the local authority for the whole community, some for members of a school and others connected with a church.

David James belongs to a church youth club. He goes to church regularly with his family and heard announcements about the youth club's meetings on Sundays after evening service. He went to a few meetings, decided he liked them – and stayed.

The activities are many and varied – sometimes in the church hall and at others in the home of one of the leaders. They have discussions on current affairs or some aspect of the church and its teachings or about a controversial television programme. Sometimes there's a speaker – perhaps a visiting preacher who has been at St. Mary's Church that day, or a missionary or someone who follows a different religion.

On the less serious side, there are games – table tennis, snooker, monopoly – or the group might just chat and listen to records.

David's youth club at St. Mary's, Hitchin, has a reputation in the local 'Youth Speaks' competition organised each year by the town's Rotary Club. St. Mary's have done very well in recent years, winning a number of times. David would like to take part, but is a little nervous of the standard that has been set by his older friends in the club.

In the summer there's a week's holiday and David went on the last one to the Diocesan Centre in the Lake District.

David enjoys the youth club. There are things to do – if you want to take part – but it's quite informal and he finds it fills his Sunday evenings.

David James enjoys camping with the Church Youth Club.

David Saint tests your wits as he asks you to . . .

Name the Patrol!

Illustrations by Cecil

Here's a Patrol who like to make it difficult for other people to work out who they are!

When you've solved the riddle of the names, see how other Scouts in your Patrol get on — and then make up a similar quiz using the names of Scouts in your own Patrol . . . and try it on the folk at home!

The Patrol Leader

The Patrol Leader wears his name on his scarf — but it's up to you to fill in the letters to find out what it is!
The answer to each of the following clues is a three-letter word. The last letters of the answers to (1) to (7) spell out his first name: the first letters of the answers to (8) to (14) spell out his surname.

(1) Hot drink.
(2) Move quickly.
(3) Scouts might store equipment in one.
(4) Left after camp fire.
(5) Rush to and . . .
(6) For litter.
(7) What to do with a wet towel.
(8) Number 13 comes in this.
(9) For breathing.
(10) To help you find your way.
(11) For hearing.
(12) A beam of sunlight.
(13) For greasing an engine.
(14) Between ENE and NE.

Assistant Patrol Leader

His name is an anagram of 'Jets on spere'. And his first name has five letters.

Third Scout

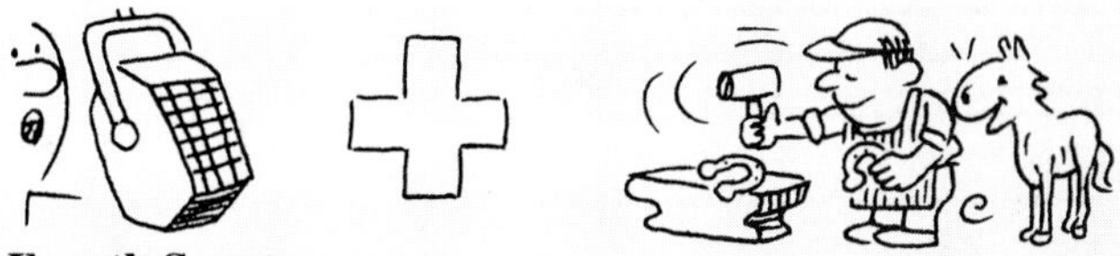

Fourth Scout

His first name is 14 2 19 12 and his second name is 3 2 12 6 19.

Fifth Scout

Sixth Scout

Turn to page 63 for the answers

Another puzzle — and this time David Saint says . . .

It's the LAW!

You know the Scout Law – but can you remember it word for word . . . and in the right order?

The Scout Law is here in the word square. Starting at the top left-hand corner, see how long it takes you to work your way to the finish. No letter may be used twice: the next letter is always in a square touching the one before it – but it might be in any direction.

Mark your trail in light pencil and test yourself against a stop watch – then challenge your friends to see if they can beat your time.

And don't look up the Scout Law until you've finished!

Solution on page 63.

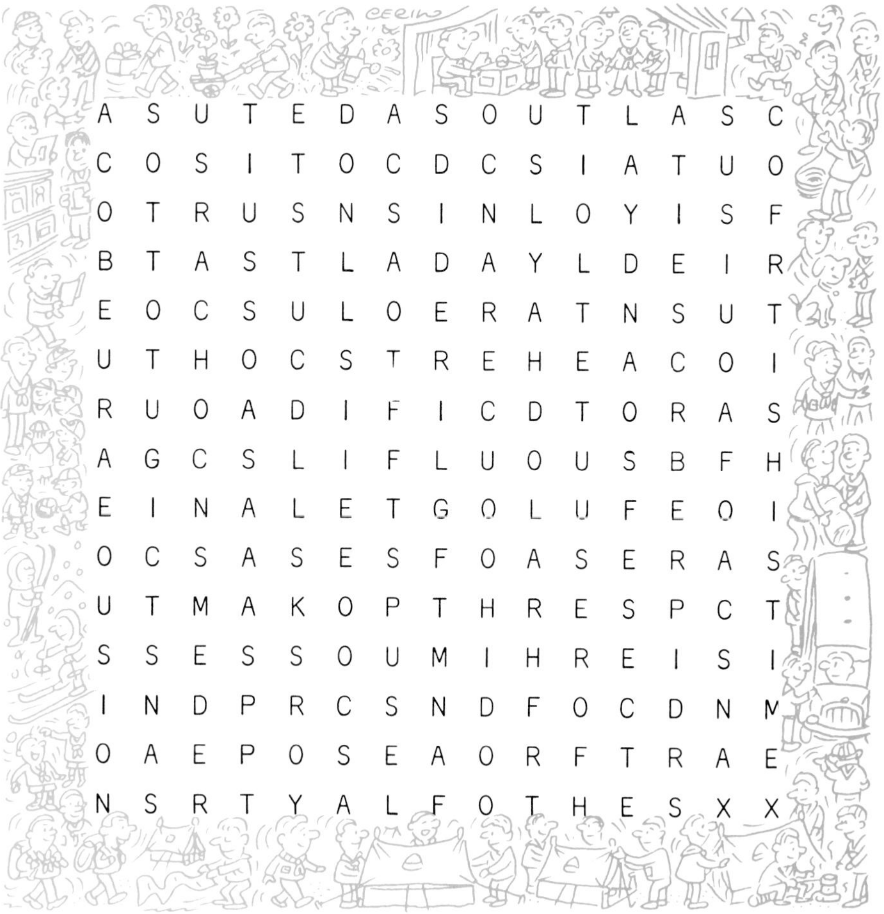

A	S	U	T	E	D	A	S	O	U	T	L	A	S	C
C	O	S	I	T	O	C	D	C	S	I	A	T	U	O
O	T	R	U	S	N	S	I	N	L	O	Y	I	S	F
B	T	A	S	T	L	A	D	A	Y	L	D	E	I	R
E	O	C	S	U	L	O	E	R	A	T	N	S	U	T
U	T	H	O	C	S	T	R	E	H	E	A	C	O	I
R	U	O	A	D	I	F	I	C	D	T	O	R	A	S
A	G	C	S	L	I	F	L	U	O	U	S	B	F	H
E	I	N	A	L	E	T	G	O	L	U	F	E	O	I
O	C	S	A	S	E	S	F	O	A	S	E	R	A	S
U	T	M	A	K	O	P	T	H	R	E	S	P	C	T
S	S	E	S	S	O	U	M	I	H	R	E	I	S	I
I	N	D	P	R	C	S	N	D	F	O	C	D	N	M
O	A	E	P	O	S	E	A	O	R	F	T	R	A	E
N	S	R	T	Y	A	L	F	O	T	H	E	S	X	X

Think you have difficulties? Denys J. Branch meets a Scout who gets to Troop Meetings . . .

THE HARD WAY!

"It's a bit of luck that I belong to two Troops – one at my school and the other near my home," said Derek Chittock, as he pushed himself along in his wheelchair.

Derek suffers from spina bifida, which prevents him from walking and doing those things that most of us take for granted. All his life he has had this problem, which has meant many stays in hospital, where the treatment he has received is both painful and unpleasant. But don't think that this gets Derek down. He has a lively sense of humour and makes light of his difficulties.

"I am taken to school each day and on Mondays we have Troop Meeting at lunchtime. Everyone in the Troop is a bit like me, but we have all the usual games and activities. If someone throws a ball and I miss, it's no use looking for someone to get it – I have to!" he said.

"Each year we go to camp and I met the Chief Scout when we were at Gilwell Park. In a way we are luckier than most Scouts, as our school Troop gets quite a lot of visitors," he added.

When Derek has to spend time in hospital he's not able to take as full a part in his local Scout Troop – the 2nd Canvey Island – as he would like. Although he uses an ordinary wheelchair at home and in school, Derek has a motor-driven chair for outdoors. It's powered by electricity and, "as long as someone is with me to help at road crossings, I can 'drive' myself to Scouts," said Derek.

And he's not left out of other activities at home, either. "With the help of my brothers and parents, I have a weekly newspaper delivery round. I carry the papers, but the others have to push them through the letterboxes!"

Derek says little about the one thing that makes him – and all who know him – very proud. A few years ago while he was staying in hospital having some unpleasant treatment, he had a visitor who represented the Chief Scout. For his gallantry and good humour over a long period in hospital Derek was presented with the Medal for Meritorious Conduct – an award he thoroughly deserves.

Derek Chittock at home on Canvey Island, Essex, with his father.

QUIZ AND PUZZLE ANSWERS

EMERGENCY! Pages 4, 5 and 6

Here's how we would suggest each emergency is handled. How did you make out and — equally important — how did the rest of your Patrol do when you showed the emergencies on pages 4, 5 and 6 to them?

Every emergency will be different and what you do first on one occasion, might not necessarily be the right thing if you meet something similar again. Looking at pictures and suggesting solutions is one thing, but it's no substitute for first aid training under expert instructors. If your Troop or District does not already do so, why not suggest that first aid training is a priority? Your Patrol Leaders' Council might discuss this and, with expert help, take members of the Troop through the first aid requirements in the training scheme.

In compiling these suggested approaches to each emergency, we are grateful to the British Red Cross Society, the Royal Life Saving Society and the Royal Society for the Prevention of Accidents for their valued assistance and advice.

1) Car crash!

(a) There are two of you — so one should cycle immediately to telephone for an ambulance and to get adult help. Cycle to the nearest house or telephone box.

(b) Switch off the car engine to reduce the danger of fire.

(c) If the driver is unconscious, ensure that his airway is clear of any obstruction that might impede his breathing. Do not move him unless it is essential. If the passenger on the ground is also unconscious, he too should be placed in the recovery position.

(d) If the passenger is conscious — or regains consciousness — and is able to move out of danger, assist him to do so. Otherwise, leave him where he is.

(e) Warn motorists coming in both directions by putting items of clothing down on the roadway some distance from the scene of the accident. If any cars come along, flag them down. Ask any adults with first aid training to help and suggest that others take on traffic control until the police or ambulance crew arrive on the scene. Keep the traffic moving to make it easier for the emergency services to reach the area.

(f) Continue to ensure that the driver and passenger are breathing freely. Keep them warm, using your coat or whatever else is available.

2) Accident!

(a) Send someone to telephone for an ambulance and to get adult help.

(b) Lay the Scout down and raise his arm high to reduce blood flow. You need to keep him warm for he could suffer from shock, so if there are coats or blankets handy let him lie on these and cover him lightly, too. Put something behind his head as a pillow.

(c) You will need to control the bleeding and to do this you should hold his arm higher than his heart to reduce the blood flow. If the bleeding is very severe, place a pad of clean bandage over the wound and apply direct pressure on the pad (and, therefore, onto the wound), keeping the arm higher than the heart all the while.

(d) Reassure the Scout until medical help arrives.

3) Fire!

(a) Use the water in the buckets to douse the fire in the tent.

(b) If the wind is strong and there's danger of sparks from the fire blowing onto other tents, use some water to douse the fire itself, too.

(c) What you do next depends on how far the rest of the Patrol have gone from the camp site to collect wood. If they are near at hand, get them back to the site. Otherwise, you must take whatever precautions are necessary to prevent other tents catching light. Getting the fire in the fireplace out must be a priority — but if sparks have already blown onto other tents you may feel that they require your attention next. Pull out the main guylines so that the tents collapse onto the ground — then remove equipment from inside.

(d) If tents are burning fiercely, don't go near or inside them. Run for adult help. Do not go into a burning tent to rescue possessions or equipment. They can be replaced — you could be badly burned.

4) Help!

On no account should you jump in to rescue the boy — however strong a swimmer you may be. You do not know the strength of the currents that are sweeping him downstream and you could both be caught up in the currents.

There are four words to remember on an occasion like this: 'reach, thrown, wade, row'.

Try first to reach him from the bank — if there's a pole or stick that you can hold out for him to clutch, so much the better.

If this doesn't work or if he is too far out into the stream, fetch the lifebelt and throw this downriver (*immediately* in front of the person in the water) so that he is swept towards it (and so that the lifebelt is not swept tantilisingly out of

reach). If this fails, go for adult help. Telephone for the police and then go back to the river bank and follow on foot until help arrives.

If the water becomes shallow enough, you could try to wade out towards the boy. If you do wade out, have something in your hand for the boy to get hold of (a stick or something similar): do *not* make contact by hand. If there's a rowing boat tied to the bank, use this. But whatever you do, don't endanger yourself. One person in trouble is enough. For example, if you are holding a stick out towards the boy from the bank, make sure that you don't topple over into the water yourself, and hold onto something firmly with the other hand so that the boy does not pull you in after him.

5) Break-in!

(a) Don't shout or draw attention to yourself.

(b) Don't try to tackle the man yourself.

(c) Make a note of the car registration number and make sure you know the address of the house. If you catch a long enough glimpse of the man, make a mental note of what he's wearing, but don't delay . . .

'What sort of person would take the team's goal posts?'

'Air traffic control reports gales of a hundred miles an hour . . .'

(d) Go to the nearest telephone box or house and call the police.

(e) Unless the police tell you to do something else, return to a spot near the house and keep watch until the police arrive, noting if the car drives off which direction it takes.

6) Danger!

Get adult help as quickly as possible. Don't run down the line or on the track towards the signal box (which could endanger you and cause an accident if there's an oncoming train). Go by road towards the signal box, but if you pass a house or telephone box before you reach the signal box, telephone the police from there. Otherwise advise the signal box keeper. Then return to the spot where you saw the children with any adult help. If the timber has been placed on the line, don't remove it yourself — with adult help stand well back from the track lower down the line and attempt to attract the attention of the driver of any train that comes along that line. Keep off the line — it could be electrified or you could slip and fall.

'This one boiled his rice!'

A Knotty Problem?

Page 19

Here are the answers to the anagrams. 'Mafeking' is the town we were after — where a British force under Baden-Powell, the Scouts founder, was beseiged (1899-1900) during the Boer War for seven months and successfully relieved.

								*													
1						T	I	M	B	E	R		H	I	T	C	H				
2						D	I	A	G	O	N	A	L		L	A	S	H	I	N	G
3								F	R	A	P	P	I	N	G		T	U	R	N	
4						S	H	E	E	T		B	E	N	D						
5			R	E	E	F		K	N	O	T										
6	C	L	O	V	E		H	I	T	C	H										
7			R	O	L	L	I	N	G		H	I	T	C	H						
8						F	I	G	U	R	E		O	F		E	I	G	H	T	

JAD'S QUIZ
Pages 44, 45 and 46

1. The King, in A. A. Milne's poem *The King's Breakfast.*
2. Lady Day, Midsummer Day, Michaelmas Day, and Christmas Day (25th December) are the four Quarter Days in England and Wales. (Scotland has different Quarter Days.)
3. (a) Norfolk; (b) County Down; (c) Dyfed; (d) Cumbria; (e) Devon.
4. The little Eskimo is the big Eskimo's daughter.
5. (a) The *Beagle* was the ship on which Charles Darwin made the journey that led him to develop his theory of evolution. (b) The *Discovery* was Captain Scott's ship on his expeditions to the Antarctic. (c) When the *Forfarshire* was wrecked off the Northumberland coast, Grace Darling and her father rescued many of its crew. (d) The *Golden Hind* (originally called the *Pelican*) was the ship in which Sir Francis Drake sailed around the world. (e) *HMS Hermes* was the flagship of the Falklands task force in 1982. (f) The *Santa Maria* (accompanied by the *Nina* and the *Pinta*) was the ship in which Columbus first sailed to America.
6. U = 92; these are the atomic numbers of carbon, hydrogen, oxygen and uranium.
7. (a) *Campfire's Burning*; (b) *John Brown's Body*; (c) *The Quartermaster's Stores*.
8. The Gunners (Arsenal) play at Highbury; the Rams (Derby County) at the Baseball Ground; the Pilgrims (Plymouth Argyle) at Home Park; the Dons (Aberdeen) at Pittodrie Stadium; and the Canaries (Norwich City) at Carrow Road.
9. You could do all sorts of thing — these are popular makes of microcomputer.
10. It still takes five minutes if you put them in the saucepan together.
11. (a) Germany (or Austria or Switzerland); (b) Wales; (c) France (or Switzerland or Belgium); (d) Spain (or parts of South America); (e) Russia.
12. During World War II, a corpse was dressed in the uniform of a Marines officer and floated ashore, carrying several forged documents to deceive the Germans about the Allied invasion plans. (See the book *The Man Who Never Was*.)
13. These are the real names of Big Daddy (the wrestler), John Wayne (the actor), Cliff Richard (the singer), John Paul II (the Pope) and Eric Morecambe and Ernie Wise (the comedians).
14. (a) rowing; (b) tug-of-war.
15. Neither can swim at all — they are both dead, smoked herring!
16. (a) rain; (b) snow; (c) fog; (d) gale; (e) thunderstorm.
17. If you count the letters in each word (and put in a decimal point) you get 3.14159265358989 — the approximate value of π, used in calculating areas and circumferences of circles.
18. James, Charles and Elizabeth each have two — they are the numbers of Kings and Queens of these names. (The answer is different in Scotland!)
19. Each half is four metres long if the plank is cut lengthwise!
20. (a) sheet bend, used for joining two ropes; (b) figure-of-eight knot, used as a 'stopper' at the end of a rope; (c) clove hitch, used to fasten a rope around a pole; (d) fisherman's knot, used for joining wet or slippery ropes; (e) sheepshank, generally used to shorten a rope at its middle.
21. The Jumblies, in the poem by Edward Lear.
22. You would get snails, fish soup, frogs' legs, and chips.
23. If John spoke, he would tell the truth and say 'I am John'; if James spoke, he would lie and say 'I am John' (or Fred, or anything except James). Neither of them would claim to be James, so the person speaking now must be lying — it is James who is speaking to you.
24. The cork costs ½p (and the bottle 10½p).

'We're nearly there – and there's still no sign of the Yeti?'

'But we gave on Sunday!'

'And here is some late news which concerns all Scouts . . .'